Touched by Elohim

The True Story of My Murder and Resurrection

MICHAEL JAMES LONGI

Published by Touched by Elohim LLC

Paperback ISBN: 979-8-9901414-1-4
Hardcover ISBN: 979-8-9901414-0-7
Ebook ISBN: 979-8-9901414-2-1

Cover and interior design by Jess LaGreca, Mayfly Design

Library of Congress Catalog Number: 2024903541
First Printing: 2024
Printed in the United States of America

Contents

Dedication

I would like to dedicate this book to Florence Fuimarello, Kimberly Toy, and Elohim.

Disclaimer

While every effort has been made to ensure the accuracy of the information presented in this book at the time of its publication, the publisher and the author make no warranties or representations, express or implied, regarding the completeness, reliability, or suitability of the content for any particular purpose. They disclaim any liability for any errors, inaccuracies, omissions, or inconsistencies that may be found within. The publisher and author shall not be held responsible for any loss, damage, or disruption resulting from such errors or omissions, whether they arise from negligence, accident, or any other cause.

Furthermore, it is essential to note that no person mentioned in this book should be presumed guilty unless proven so in a court of law. The events recounted in this book are the author's recollection of personal experiences, and to protect the privacy and identities of certain individuals, some names have been altered.

CHAPTER 1

My Death

I died in West Las Vegas at age 46.

It was Wednesday, February 10, 2016. The time was 10:00 a.m.

The spot where I died is nothing special. The intersection of West Charleston Boulevard and South Town Center Drive was a few blocks from the fancy Red Rock Resort, home to the largest casino on that side of "Lost Wages." I was nearby at a four-way stop in the parking lot of a typical shopping center that contained a grocery store, a bank, a gas station, an Asian restaurant, a tanning salon, and a place to get your nails done. There was a McDonald's and a Starbucks to my right, a Del Taco to my left. Towering palm trees stood all around.

At the moment I died, I was fully stopped at that four-way parking lot intersection, behind the wheel of my little Lexus GS 350.

Except for the palm trees and the nearby casino, the parking lot could have been anywhere in the United States.

Right before I died, I looked left, making sure there was no cross traffic before turning. I was heading to a meeting regarding an IRS audit, but I was ravenously hungry and wanted a breakfast burrito from Del Taco.

What happened next was pure horror.

A violent shaking overtook my body like nothing I'd felt before, like I was riding a bucking bronco in a rodeo but amplified exponentially.

My mouth made a wailing noise. I would understand later that this was the sound of my soul being separated from my body. This is what I would learn to call a death wail. The wailing came with an all-encompassing pain—as much pain as if I had taken a dive off a high-rise and landed on concrete. The pain lasted only a moment but felt like an eternity.

There was a blinding, magnificent light. It was a living light and part of a universe of consciousness. Other smaller lights surrounded me as well.

I found myself looking around—*everywhere*.

I was scared and panicked.

I was looking for my body, but I couldn't find it. I was not *of* my body. *Where's my body? Where's my body? Why can't I find my body?*

After a moment, a clear thought came to me. *Wait. If I don't have a body, I must be dead.*

I waited for my cognition to disappear like smoke in the wind—after all, I was dead. The opposite started happening. I was growing more aware of the nature of the universe.

I was aware of interacting with other spirits that looked like balls of light. I was no longer of this earth. I realized I was also in a spirit state. It was then that many secrets of the universe were revealed.

We come from a universe of conscious thought. It is consciousness that creates the physical universe.

And I realized that I was *thinking*—that I was processing all of this.

The thought was clear as a bell.

Wow, I thought. *This is phenomenal. This is just like on last week's episode of* Ancient Aliens. *I'm really hardwired into this universe.*

Then, the most narcissistic thought crossed my mind.

This means the universe is here for me—and I am not here because of the universe.

I realized in those few seconds that God is that universe of pure conscious thought. It felt as if he was cradling me in his arms. He was all around me.

I no longer felt any pain or suffering. It felt as if I was eternally at peace.

It's important to know that I had never used God in conversation. But in this moment, it felt as if I could travel from one end of the universe to the other by pure conscious thought. I realized it is God's consciousness that creates the reality we are in.

Life is just consciousness within consciousness.

That's all it is.

This universe is here for us. We really are in a matrix.

I realized consciousness existed way before any physical universe. I always had a hard time grappling with the concept that life came from a rock. After all, that's all the Earth is, a rock. How could life spring from a rock?

It can't. *Consciousness* existed first.

But I wasn't ready to die.

. . . .

It was as though I had the choice of staying in that immortal state or returning to the physical universe. I started thinking of all the big business deals I was involved with and felt the need to get back to the physical universe and attend to them. I was about to broker some really monster transactions. I was closing on my new house with an amazing view of the Valley. I was going through a routine IRS audit with my pension plan. I also had my two Labrador dogs at home. Who would look after them? I had to get back. I was not ready to die.

Even so, the powerful feeling of eternal peace made the lure of death hard to resist. But I still realized I had to go back.

Life was not finished for me yet, and I willed myself back into my body. When I say willed myself back, that is an understatement. I started screaming hysterically, "I am not ready to die!"

I felt consciousness enter my crown and then take over all my limbs. It was a powerful sucking sensation, like in the episodes of *Ancient Aliens* where they talk about the soul entering the crown at birth.

It seemed like I was in the afterlife for several minutes, but no time had elapsed in the physical universe. I was back in my car with my foot on the brake at the stop sign.

I heard a voice from the heavens: *This was no accident, this was meant to kill you, this had something to do with the Sattari family.*

It was the voice of God. The voice was pure thunder and lightning. It was no regular voice. It was powerful. It was as if the entire universe of pure conscious thought—the entire afterlife—was speaking to me.

God's voice was followed by a chorus of laughing voices that faded off to the heavens. It was all those balls of light—those angels, those minions, God's whole entourage—laughing at me.

I felt upset. I became angry and defiant. But, at least at first, I was not afraid.

I immediately said "bullshit" to that voice. I said, "I love everyone in the Sattari family. None of this shit just happened. None of this is real."

I started to recall how I was informally adopted by the Sattaris. I loved everyone in that family. I *knew* it was not them; they could not be the ones behind this horror.

The Sattaris were a powerful Persian family from Iran. I was brokering their entire land portfolio, worth millions of dollars. We were about to go into escrow on twenty acres near Hualapai and Farm. In fact, I was in the middle of several major land deals.

My foot was firmly on the brake of my Lexus as I said out loud, "I want proof."

You have heard the expression from people in near-death experiences that their life flashed before their eyes? That they felt they had seen everything that happened to them in their lives, in a brief moment?

It's true. My life flashed before my eyes in a fraction of a second. It was more of a pulling from my consciousness. I felt the universe judge me, and a chill flashed down my spine. Now I felt fear!

I experienced a powerful sensation—that whatever entity had judged me would control what happened to me in the next life. When I died, I'd seen myself. In fact, I saw everything.

I saw that I had never committed to a family. I suddenly saw who I was, and I saw all the things I had stood for. It wasn't a pretty picture. God was not pleased that I had said "bullshit" to what he was telling me. I immediately feared not for my life, but for my immortal soul.

This made no sense. You don't die in a parking lot.

And the timing was all wrong. I was considered one of the few Land Gods of the Las Vegas Valley. I had spent years as one of the most high-profile real estate agents in the fast-growing city. My specialty was land, raw land. I was a mover and a shaker. I was independently wealthy. I had come so far. I had served in the U.S. Navy during the Gulf War. I worked throwing bags for Southwest Airlines. I had worked hard to get to the top of the real estate business in Las Vegas. I had survived the market crash of 2008, and I rode the wave back to the top.

The first thing I noticed, back in the physical universe, was that a giant full-ton Chevrolet 3500 Silverado pickup truck had plowed into the rear of my car. There had been no sound of brakes. I got out of my car, grabbing my neck. The driver was already standing outside my car.

I stood there and could feel changes inside me too; my brain became totally rewired, as if new parts of my brain were getting blood and other parts of my brain were now closed off.

My company's 401(k) plan was going through a routine audit at the time, and I had some anxiety since it was my first experience with the IRS. That had been my focus. But right after my consciousness returned, it was like I was going through a hundred audits all at once.

The first thing the pickup truck driver said was, "This was an accident—I didn't even see you."

What a peculiar thing for someone to say, I thought. *When is a car wreck not an accident?*

I tried not to think of the voice of God and what I'd heard. I just wanted to move on with my life.

The truck driver insisted on calling an ambulance. He must have insisted at least a dozen times. I kept refusing. I didn't have the time.

I was working on two major deals. The first was the opportunity to sell a pig farm owned by my friend, Robert Combs. I'd been cultivating my relationship with Bob Combs for over a decade. I had made a huge loan to help Bob Combs stay afloat, and my generosity with that note had sealed my standing as an enterprising, hardworking person who would mutually benefit as Combs' trusted broker.

In addition, I was about to broker the deal for the Sattari family on the twenty acres at Hualapai and Farm—another contract that I had been chasing for years.

There was a lot of good going on in my life, including my passion for mixed martial arts. I was about to take my blue belt test in Brazilian jiu-jitsu from the world champion, Robert Drysdale, and a kenpo test with Kenpo Master Jeff Speakman that would earn me another stripe on my brown belt on my way to getting my black belt.

I had no time to be hurt, and I certainly had no time to die with everything going on in my life. And I had no time for an ambulance.

I told him I simply wanted to get his information and move on with my day. I did not want him calling the shots.

We moved our vehicles from the intersection and into the parking lot in front of the Del Taco. When I realized how massive his pickup truck was, I was stunned at what I had survived.

I realized almost immediately that the only reason why I had lived was because of the nightly neck crunches recommended to me by Robert Drysdale, who was once referred to by *Vice* magazine as "America's jiu-jitsu superhero." Four months before the wreck, Drysdale had insisted I do thirty minutes of neck crunches every night in preparation for my blue belt test. Drysdale told me he always noticed how I tapped out of choke holds. He said he wanted to make my neck indestructible. It worked. My neck could flex, and biceps would snap off it like rubber bands.

The driver gave me his insurance information. Suddenly, he became one of the nicest people on earth. Out of the blue, he asked me if I would say that my car was moving when I reported it to my insurance company.

I thought, *this guy just killed me, and now he wants me to commit insurance fraud.* I felt a paralyzing fear.

"No," I said, "that's not what happened." I told him that I was fully braked when he plowed into me.

The man became violently confrontational. He started screaming, and I feared for my life. I wasn't afraid of defending myself given all my mixed martial arts training, but I didn't want to risk the fact that he might be armed. *Fuck this guy*, I thought. *What a total creeper.* God did say this was no accident and was meant to kill me. I would not put it past the driver to be carrying a gun.

I was numb. I had no idea how much damage might have been done to my body or to my brain. I only knew I had things to do.

I also knew I had been forever changed. It would take weeks and months for those changes to become apparent, for me to understand what had happened, and for me to realize that I had been touched by God.

· · · ·

I later learned from doctors that rear-end wrecks are exponentially more deadly when the car in front is fully stopped. Not only was my car fully stopped, but he plowed into me without braking. This guy knew exactly what he was doing and how to make it deadly.

It was attempted murder.

As I drove my damaged vehicle away, I said a silent prayer to God. I was still defiant. *God, the insurance fraud the driver wanted me to commit proves nothing. I want more proof than that.* I felt like challenging God. Even though the driver clearly tried to kill me, I wanted more proof this had something to do with the Sattari family.

A powerful thought overcame me: *There will be more murder attempts when I enter litigation, and those responsible will be revealed.*

I could not believe what I just felt. I knew I had changed in many ways, and it seemed like my intuition was amplified. The thought did not seem to originate from my own consciousness. It was a disturbing ominous waring I was not going to forget.

Later that night, I had a feeling I was forgetting to do something important.

When I thought of the car wreck, I burst out crying. Why was I so emotional? Why was I so scatterbrained? I should have known anyone going from life to death, back to life, would endure physical trauma. I put the wreck out of my mind as a safety defense mechanism.

I reported to my insurance company, and then realized I had forgotten to get the driver's license of the guy who hit me. I had his insurance information, however. And I had photos of his truck.

That evening, I continued to feel disoriented. I was trying to make sense of my new universe and all I had learned and been shown by God.

Later that night, somewhere between sleep and wakefulness, I heard a loud whisper:

"Your life will never be the same."

Startled, I jumped out of bed.

Did I hear those words or imagine them?

I fell asleep around 9:00 p.m. and then was wide awake minutes later. It still felt like the wreck had just occurred.

Another sign things were different was that my dog, Star, insisted on sleeping next to me as a third pillow. Before, she had slept at the foot of my bed.

· · · ·

They say that when a man wants to find God, he climbs the highest mountain. I had first found God, and he found me at the age of 12 on top of one of Colorado's highest peaks in the middle of a blizzard.

They also say that when a man wants to find his soul, he wanders the Judean Desert for forty days and forty nights like Moses and Jesus Christ did. I had found my soul when I travelled to the other side during that long moment—when I could see all of time—the past and the future after I died violently. I knew what it was like to go from life to death, back to life, never losing consciousness. How many people does that happen to?

I knew what it felt like to be murdered in the blink of an eye.

Like the whisper said, my life would never be the same.

CHAPTER 2

Early Wanderings

I was one guy before the car wreck.

I was another guy after.

The first version of Michael James Longi was a distinctly different person, both inside and out. The damage to my insides wasn't immediately apparent.

There are details around the crash that won't make much sense without some background from my business dealings.

So before diving into the bizarre elements around the wreck—along with the amazing coincidences that saved my life *and* proved that it was attempted murder—let me give you an idea of who I was before I decided to stop for breakfast at Del Taco.

At least, that is, the key highlights.

I was born on December 1, 1969, at Offutt Air Force Base outside Omaha, Nebraska. My parents were both enlisted in the U.S. Air Force and later became officers. I was the oldest child. My sister Mary was born a year later, and Kathy followed four years after that. My brother Joshua is seventeen years younger than me and, even later, my parents adopted my sister Sara, who is actually my sister Mary's daughter.

As a kid, all I knew was change. After Omaha, I went to live with my grandmother for close to a year. Then it was Mississippi, where Mary was born. Next was England for two years. At 5, I was in San Antonio for three years.

While living in San Antonio, we took a trip north to Fort Worth and were staying at a resort near Six Flags Over Texas. It was the summer of 1976. My newest sister, Kathy, was just 22 months old.

I was hanging out with my mom, dad, and sister Mary at the swimming pool.

"Where's Kathleen?" I asked.

At first, my parents didn't seem to be very worried. At all. I started looking for her. My intuition was telling me to be alarmed. A profound thought came into my head: I needed to go to the kids' swimming pool. Apparently, Kathy had fallen down while walking in the shallow water and had slipped to the bottom of the pool. She didn't know how to get back up. In horror, I saw my baby sister at the bottom of the swimming pool, arms and legs flailing.

I jumped in and pulled her to safety. I had followed my intuition when I was only 6 years old. When I pulled her out of the pool, she immediately coughed up all the water she had swallowed and started crying. She had been very close to death. I would learn later that drowning victims often die on their second gulp of water. She'd had one.

My parents should have known better than to let little kids play by the pool without keeping an eye on them, but my quick action and intuition saved my sister's life. I reminded my parents on a regular basis—especially when I was in hot water—that I had saved their daughter's life.

My father and mother usually treated me well, but from time to time, I suffered the occasional dose of physical abuse and beatings with belts and other objects. My earliest recollection was at the age of 4, I got cracked in the skull with a metal object for carrying on about something. My father ran out of the house and bought me a child's book as a gift to make up for it. After the beatings, he would always tell me that his father beat on him a lot worse than he was whipping me. He was trying to pretend he was somehow a better parent than his father by telling me this, but all I knew was that the beatings were very traumatic. It was brutal. The whippings left welts and broke skin.

Ours was not a harmonious household—at least when it came to me. I still loved and cared about my mom and dad very much and wanted to make them proud.

. . . .

When I was a child, we were ostensibly Catholics. We went to church on a fairly regular basis, and I attended Sunday School for an hour every week. In Ohio, I even attended a Catholic school. At first, my family was passionate about going to church. I received my first communion at 7 years old.

But then, I was baptized as a Mormon in January 1982 when I had just turned 12 years old. To me, there are good people of God in the Catholic Church, and there are good people of God in the Mormon Church. But one thing I liked about the Mormon Church, or the Church of Jesus Christ of Latter-day Saints as it's known, is that you can ascend to Godhood. I believe that. We have an immortal soul. All of us on Earth carry the spark of Godhood in us. If our immortal soul cannot die, how can we not be gods? In 2016, when I physically died, I saw all religions in the afterlife. I didn't see only the Mormon Church or the Catholic Church or Buddhism or Hinduism or Islam. It was all there, intertwined.

. . . .

It was while living in Woodmoor Colorado that I had my first encounter with death—on a mountaintop. In a blizzard.

In Woodmoor, as a 12-year-old, I liked the Mormon Church for another reason. They had a deep connection with the Boy Scouts. In fact, the Mormon Church had a formal partnership with the Scouts that lasted for more than 100 years before they separated for allowing women to join. The Boy Scouts then ran into huge scandals for sex abuse beginning in about 2010. The Scout troops I belonged to were led by ethical people, and this type of stuff was not going on.

The great thing about the Boy Scout connection is that you're camping one week and canoeing the next. For someone who had just turned

12, it was fun. As a kid in Ohio, I had joined the Cub Scouts, and I knew I liked all the activities. As a young man growing up, they teach you a strong set of values and keep you on the straight and narrow path. Later, in Florida, we would go snorkeling in the Florida Keys, deep sea fishing, and canoeing in the Everglades. I was very active after we moved to Florida (though I hated camping in the Everglades because the mosquitoes seemed to feast on my O-negative blood type.) I stayed with the Mormon Church through my first year in Alabama, in ninth grade, and then kind of separated from it. I made it through three years because my parents made me, but no teenager in their right mind wants to go to church for three hours every Sunday (and most adults in their right mind don't want to do that either).

My father had been baptized into the Mormon Church through one of his cadets by the name of Ted Parsons. My dad was the one who baptized the rest of us.

In May 1982, four months after I was baptized, our Boy Scout troop was planning a two-day expedition to the summit of Pikes Peak, which is the towering and famous 14,111-foot mountain that rises to the west of Colorado Springs. The group going up was Scouts and leaders with tight Mormon connections and lots of camping and hiking experience. I really wanted to be part of them.

The Scout leaders weren't going to let me join them. They said I was too small. I was devastated. I cried to my dad about it. I was determined. My dad raised hell. Next, the Scoutmasters claimed I didn't have the right type of gear, like snowshoes and survival gear. In April, there is usually a heavy mantle of snow that remains on Pikes Peak, so good winter gear was required. The truth is that my father was a bit on the cheap side, especially when it came to me, and we did not have good equipment.

My dad's complaints worked, and he went out and bought me the proper gear. I ended up climbing up the trail with everyone. At the halfway point, there's a rest area with a small group of cabins, and a young hiker told us that a big snowstorm was on the way. At the end of that first day, nearly two-thirds of those on the journey headed back down. They didn't want anything to do with the coming storm.

I stayed. I was determined to finish. But by the middle of the second day, as we reached the tree line, it started to snow. *Hard.*

Foolishly, I didn't eat my lunch. I wanted to save it. I started lagging behind. And struggling. It was brutal. I thought I would die. I started praying for God and Jesus. "Actually, I wasn't just praying for them, I was screaming for them." I glanced down, and I could see entire mountains below me that looked like ant beds. So small were they compared to where I was it was a staggering realization how high up I was. I couldn't believe it. As the snow was piling up; I was trudging through white powder up to my waist. Right before the top, it felt like it might be easier to climb on all fours.

After a grueling struggle, we reached the summit. To the left of me was a bottomless chasm below, to the right was a restaurant and a gift shop. In the summer months, the road is open and there's a scenic train that comes up from the other side. There are many ways to reach the top of Pikes Peak with no effort whatsoever, but not when it's mid-spring and there's still snow up there. The store was locked. One of the Scout-masters picked the lock, and we made it inside and helped ourselves to snacks and refreshments. Another Scoutmaster called the rangers, and soon, a four-wheel drive SUV came and picked us up and drove us back down the mountain.

This was the first time God answered me—I could feel God latch onto my body and say, *we need to see what happens with this guy in life.* I had come very close to making it up that mountain but very close to dying at the same time. Somehow, after praying and crying for God, I was saved, and my life would never be the same.

A few months after that first near-death experience, we moved to a spot south of Miami. We were about one mile outside Homestead Air Force Base, which was pummeled by Hurricane Andrew in 1992. About a block down the street lived a fellow student named Billy Nida. He liked to mess around with guns, specifically, a 12-gauge shotgun that his father owned. He would put a shell in the chamber and pull the trigger, pointing it at me.

Click. Click. Click. Click. Click. Click.

Six times—nothing happened.

Finally, Billy pointed the shotgun at the ceiling and pulled the trigger. *Ka-boom!*

My ears exploded. Thank goodness the gun hadn't gone off when he had pointed it at me. I was horrified. The experience shook me to my core.

Every time I walked into his house after that, there was a white piece of paper taped over the hole in the ceiling. Billy had to make up a story to his father about how a guest at a party got drunk or something along those lines. It was a good sized hole.

That was my second near-death experience. You carry that kind of sound with you. You feel the shock and fear in your chest. I was searching everywhere for the holes in my body when the gun went off. I *freaked out.*

Billy said he was sorry. "Thank goodness you're alive or I would have had to throw your body in the canal."

Gulp.

How ironic that this was only a few months after the rugged hike on Pikes Peak when I was crying for God.

In Florida, Alabama, and when I lived in Stuttgart, Germany, my parents started bringing me to family therapy. They wanted to find a way to deal with my rebellious nature and get me to settle down, but I had no way of communicating how I was being treated at home. I felt completely trapped by my parents.

I met a kid by the name of Darren Prestwood when I first moved to Florida while staying on Homestead Air Force Base. One time, I snuck out of the house by climbing through my window to go meet Darren at a bowling alley for pizza and soda and to just mess around. I was caught. The power had gone off and come back on at our house, causing my alarm clock to beep relentlessly. I was permanently grounded. Worse, my parents removed the door to my bedroom! Can you imagine how humiliating and maddening it would be for a teenage boy to have his bedroom door removed—the sheer lack of privacy while going through puberty.

Unfortunately, Darren Prestwood died when he got thrown out of a car after it hit a tree when he was 17 years old, shortly before Hurricane Andrew hit Florida hard. When I found out later about his death, I was deeply saddened. He was my best friend when I lived in Florida. I felt a deep sense of sadness for his family who I became close with while living there.

As a military kid, you get used to moving around—not that I liked it. My family relocated every two years. I was always the new kid in class, often long after the school year had started. All the friendships and cliques were set, so I had to learn how to meet friends quickly. Meet friends, that is, and *make* friends. I think that contributed to my becoming a good salesperson later in life. I had to be fearless and gregarious and easygoing.

Next, we moved to a small town called Prattville, Alabama. My folks were stationed in Montgomery, twelve miles away. This was a stark contrast from living thirty miles south of Miami.

One day, I was riding a Honda ATC 110 three-wheeler on the road.

A car hit me. I flew twenty feet in the air and landed hard on my ass. I was beyond shaken.

That same year, I was traversing a steep hill, and the ATC flipped over. After I landed, I both heard and felt a crash. The three-wheeler landed on top of me, putting a monster dent in my helmet. If I had not been wearing head protection, I would have been dead. My near-death experiences were becoming as numerous as our moves.

After living in Alabama, my mom got stationed in Stuttgart, Germany, but Dad was sent to Oslo, Norway. It was while I was living in Oslo that I spent a semester at High Wycombe, in England. The American high school in Oslo only went up to tenth grade, and I was starting eleventh grade. Military brats that lived in countries that did not accommodate people grade level ended up in schools like the one in High Wycombe, England. Without getting into it, I was a little bit of a hellion in England and ended up getting pulled from the school before expulsion. Next, I ended up briefly in Stuttgart Germany, living with my mom, and then we all returned to San Antonio, when I was finishing 11th grade. San Antonio, Texas is where I graduated high school.

During all this instability and moving from town to town, one constant was my summers in Poughkeepsie, a town on the Hudson River north of New York City. My Uncle Jimmy lived there and so did my grandmother, Florence. Uncle Jimmy was one of Florence's two sons. The other was his younger brother Raymond—my father.

My grandmother helped raise me in my first year of life. She had many grandchildren, but I was her favorite. We had a special bond because of our time together.

I also became very close to her husband, Tony. He was not my biological grandfather, but he would always say I was the son he should have had. First, a bit more about my amazing grandmother. She was born in 1921 and received a "Key to the City" for her excellence in bookkeeping and business upon graduation from high school in Poughkeepsie, New York. Florence had two sons, Raymond (my father) and James. Florence and her first husband, James Longi, got a divorce when the kids were very young. (She was married to Husband #2 for a year or two before I was born.)

Her third husband, Tony, had one son. She and Tony loved horses and enjoyed going to the tracks at Saratoga and Monticello. She had a keen mind and was razor-sharp well into her nineties. She first worked at a Singer sewing machine store in Poughkeepsie, then as an office manager for a building supply store, and for many years worked for the Mid-Hudson Library. She worked until she was 80 years old.

Her husband Tony, whom I considered my grandfather, had been a World War II vet. He was a gun collector and gave me my first pellet gun when I was just a little kid. My bond with Tony Fuimarello was as special as my bond with my grandmother.

When my grandmother and grandfather visited us while we were living in Prattville, they saw my parents always yelling at me and not treating me properly. My Grandpa Tony wanted to bring me back to Poughkeepsie to raise me as his son, and my grandmother got in a fight with him, saying that wouldn't be appropriate.

Grandpa Tony passed around December of 1994, and unfortunately, Florence passed away while this book was being written. She died on March 25, 2020, at 4:20 a.m. Up until she died, we talked on the phone almost every day. She was my confidant. And she was the one family member I was the closest to, the one family member who made me feel like I had a family.

I have two biological sisters. Mary is a mother and homemaker. Kathy is retired as an officer from the U.S. Army and today audits banks for the U.S. government. My younger brother Joshua (Josh) is an assistant district attorney in San Antonio, Texas. And last but not least is Sara, who is both my adopted sister and my biological niece. They all live around San Antonio, Texas.

CHAPTER 3

The U.S. Navy

My parents woke me up early one summer morning between eleventh and twelfth grade.

"Mike—somebody's here to see you."

It was still dark outside, 4:30 a.m.

What was going on? This made no sense to me. Who would be visiting at that hour? Visiting me? I rubbed the long hair out of my eyes.

It was a recruiter from the U.S. Navy.

I knew immediately that my parents were trying to get me to move out. I wasn't the best student. I liked to skip school—I'm not going to lie. I'd skip classes with friends, and we'd goof around. Just another bunch of teenagers who didn't, at the time, see the point of school. If we had some pot, we'd smoke it. If we had beer, we'd drink it. We'd play music. I was into all the hair bands, a sub-genre of heavy metal music. Maybe all you need to know is that my first concert was Iron Maiden and Twisted Sister during Iron Maiden's Power Slave Tour in Birmingham, Alabama in 1984.

I never was held back a grade, but I wasn't into school. In all my classes, even in college, I did the bare minimum. I didn't care about making straight A's. I understood what I was being taught. Getting good grades would have been easy, but I didn't care enough to put in the work.

The Navy recruiter got me to commit. I joined up on a delayed enlistment, meaning that I would head to the U.S. Navy as soon as I graduated high school. My diploma was my ticket to military service. It was also my ticket out of my family and all the restrictions and rules and lack of freedom.

The recruiter got me to commit initially as an electrician's mate. But when my dad found out my commitment was only for three years, he called them and raised hell. My dad got them to re-sign me—for four years as an interior communications electrician. The first time I enlisted I was going to the Great Lakes Chicago area. The second time, it would be San Diego. Many years later, my father got my brother to join the Marines when he was 17, but when it was time for him to go in, he was a no-show. The sheriff came to get him, but he still refused.

I was failing my twelfth-grade English class. It was the last class of the day, so it was one I frequently skipped. My dad called up my teacher and begged and pleaded with her to pass me. He told her that if I failed, I couldn't join the Navy. She told him that my attendance was one of the worst she had ever seen.

"But," she said, "if your son can get in front of the class and recite Hamlet's 'To Be Or Not To Be' soliloquy without missing one word, I will pass him."

I was motivated. I stood in front of the class and recited all 260 words without making one mistake. The whole class, including the teacher, broke into applause and excitement. I can still remember that soliloquy to this day.

To be, or not to be, that is the question:
Whether 'tis nobler in the mind to suffer
The slings and arrows of outrageous fortune,
Or to take Arms against a Sea of troubles,
And by opposing end them: to die, to sleep . . .

Hamlet's speech goes on from there, of course, and is one of the most celebrated soliloquies ever written. Hamlet contemplates death and suicide. He bemoans the pain and unfairness of life but acknowledges that the alternative might be worse.

Of course, at the time, I had no idea that one day I would experience death, view all of the afterlife, and come back to this earth and to my mortal body and "this mortal coil." Nor did I know that I would one day have my own bouts with suicidal thoughts. At the time, the speech was a memorization test. Reciting it was my exit ticket from high school. I had no idea that I would one day understand Hamlet in a way that few other humans experience—his torment and the heavy topics he was grappling to understand.

. . . .

I got my diploma the following June, and I started my four-year hitch in August.

First, boot camp. In San Diego.

Boot camp was a big shock. We were waking up around 2:00 a.m. when we first got there. It was a lot of work. It was so exhausting that I would sleep through the academic portion of the class. My instructor, First-Class Petty Officer Slinger, noticed this. He was ready to have me do push-ups forever if, and when, I took the tests and I failed. When I took the test to graduate from boot camp, I got the highest academic score out of the entire company. I was supposed to get a promotion to E3 out of boot camp as a result, but Chief Officer Reyes gave the promotion to a recruit from the Philippines who came in right under me.

After boot camp, I was assigned to the USS Belleau Wood, nicknamed "Devil Dog," and the second ship named after the Battle of Belleau Wood in World War I. It was the third of five in a new class of general-purpose amphibious assault ships. We could deliver a U.S. Marine Corps battalion and all the needed equipment by landing craft, helicopters, or both.

My entire Navy career, other than boot camp, was spent on the Belleau Wood. My first experience was being at quarters on top of this massive flight deck the size of a football stadium. Petty Officer Amsler showed up and threw all my sheets and berthing gear on the flight deck in front of everyone because I did not make my bunk. It was humiliating.

Before, when I was just going to school, I wanted to retire in the Navy; now, I just wanted to do my time and get out.

. . . .

We sailed to Hawaii and were stationed there for a year. Next, we were supposed to go to Canada for leave and liberty when the Gulf War ("Desert Storm") broke out. Our ship got called to the Long Beach shipyards, and we were there for fifteen months. After Long Beach, it was back to San Diego.

In December 1989, I visited San Antonio on leave from the Navy. I wanted to see some old friends and my sister, Mary, because we were very close. My parents had been assigned to a U.S. Air Force Base in Seoul, Korea. My sister Mary, who was 18, refused to move with them. I was horrified to learn that she was homeless. I ended up getting her a room with the Rabideau family. I went to high school with three Rabideau kids: Buddy, Jason, and Angela. It was a great relief to find my sister a place to live while she found her way in life. It was during this trip to San Antonio that I had a fling with a woman named Teresa. Remember her name. She comes back later in the story.

The most fun I had was being assigned to shore patrol in Long Beach. For four months, my job was to drive around, go to nightclubs, pick up drunken sailors or marines, and take them back to the ship. When you worked shore patrol, you got your own room. This was so much better than being on the ship, where living quarters meant 120 people per berthing area, packed like sardines. Speaking of stinky things—it never failed: there was always at least one smelly person in every berthing area who made living conditions difficult. You had to live in triple bunk beds.

Shore patrol involved a great schedule too. Three days of work one week (working 12-hour shifts) followed by four days the next week. And repeat.

Even with shore patrol, I didn't fit into military life. My parents loved it. I did not. I don't regret going into the Navy, but it was my parents who pushed me into it. I knew it wasn't my thing. For starters, you're living paycheck to paycheck. The enlisted people who survive are the ones living on the ship because they don't have the extra living expenses. It's free. But you're living on a ship. It wasn't for me.

I know my time in the Navy shaped my life in several ways. It showed me what kind of life I did not want to pursue. I graduated with an electrical engineering degree, and the Navy took full advantage of what I had learned.

On the positive side, the Navy taught me that hard work pays off. It also allowed me to leave home at a young age and not rely on Mom and Dad. I proudly served my country honorably during the Gulf War. When you learn to rely on yourself, you become more successful.

CHAPTER 4

Family Strife

When I left the Navy, I received an honorable discharge. I was a two-time nationally decorated soldier with a Battle "E" Defense Service Medal (because our ship was in service during a war, even if we didn't see direct action).

I left the military, with pride, as a third-class petty officer. I would have tested for second-class petty officer, but for some reason, my chief in the Navy did not like it when I told him that I was officer material because both my mom and dad were officers. Some people in life do not know how to take a joke.

I decided to move back in with my mom, which lasted no more than two days before I found a room with a couple and another female in a three-bedroom apartment. When I left there, I bounced from friend apartment to friend apartment, living on couches and occasionally sleeping in my car. My mom's place was not an option. The idea of me living at home was forever finished. There was a one-month period I literally lived out of my car. I would crash my college friends' apartments to shower there.

At the time, in 1992, my mom was stationed at Nellis Air Force Base. My dad had just retired a few months before I got out from the constraints of the navy. However, he was teaching ROTC in New York. This foreshadowed his second career. Years later, my father earned his credentials to become an assistant principal and ended up becoming one, after 30 years of military service, in St Louis, Missouri.

The year 1992 was a big one in our family. My parents split up. I had no idea what was going on, but my mother was crushed. Devastated.

Just imagine—at the time, my baby brother Joshua was only five years old, and they had adopted my niece, Sara, who was even younger. In essence, my mother was raising her second family. She had retired one month short of 20 years in the military because she was a hardcore Mormon, and her sense of family focus was powerful. Had she made it to 20 years in the military, she would have been eligible for both retirement and disability benefits (she had had a hysterectomy). However, she ended up receiving only one retirement check. She had some tax benefits on her income because she had a disability rating. But she did not receive a second check like she would have if she had completed 20 years. With two little ones, it was a rough spot for her to face.

She did not know that her husband was about to divorce her. If she had known, of course, she would not have left a few days short of the 20-year mark. She was blind-sided the second she got out. At the time, she probably thought they were just living apart and would soon get back to living in the same location to raise the two new members of their family, Joshua and my niece Sara.

My mother fought my father hard over the divorce. She didn't want to grant it.

Looking back, the split-up wasn't completely unexpected. My parents fought all the time. I knew there were issues.

I remember lots of screaming between them. From the time we moved to Colorado and all the stops after that, they were always violently yelling at each other.

I knew one thing for sure—my family was dysfunctional. I knew there had to be better examples out there of loving families.

My parents ended up eventually divorcing in 1993. I ended up getting that job at Southwest Airlines the same year, which helped to keep the family together for another seven years after they divorced because my access to free travel allowed my dad to remain part of his kids' life.

My father would fly in every month or two, thanks to my job. My brother and adopted younger sister would have never gotten to know their father if not for me. It is something I am deeply proud of. I gave them four years of my life in the military and almost seven years at Southwest Airlines.

In 1992, however, I didn't know all this. I just needed a place to live. I thought about San Antonio as an option, but the state of Nevada paid a hundred dollars more per month in unemployment than Texas. And Nevada was one of the few states with no income tax. I felt there was more opportunity in the Silver State and felt a calling to make it my home.

My parents were sending a message: I had to make it on my own. Either make it in life or be homeless.

If they had taken me in, I would have been pampered. I would not have become the entrepreneur in life I became.

Instead, I had no safety net. In retrospect, it was a terrific gift to be put in a situation where I had to sink or swim on my own.

At the time, my parents had a house in North Las Vegas in a master-planned community called El Dorado. This was the first master-planned community in North Las Vegas. The area was known for one thing—the way it smelled.

The stench was from R.C. Farms, owned by Bob Combs. Even though the farm was a mile from my house, the smell drifted in at least once a week.

It was a pig farm.

Little did I realize, at the time, how big a role that pig farm would play in my career—as well as with the attempt on my life.

In fact, the pig farm would become directly—and deeply—intertwined with my murder.

CHAPTER 5

First Taste of Employment after the Navy

For nearly a year after my stint in the Navy, I collected unemployment and hung out. I didn't do much. When unemployment ran out, I got a job in medical sales—pharmaceuticals. The job was in a call center. I spent all day on the phone. I knew I could do better, so I put in an application to work for Southwest Airlines at McCarran International Airport. I knew that the airline industry liked to hire military veterans with honorable discharges. I thought I had a good chance.

Later, I found out that a guy named Chris had tried to contact me about an interview, but I missed the call because I was in a college class. Once I knew he had tried to get hold of me, I called every day for a job from that day forward. It was my persistence that won out.

Finally, success. It was the summer of 1993. A job offer came in from Southwest Airlines. I accepted immediately. Once trained, I did a little bit of everything the airline needed. I was a ramp agent. I marshaled in the aircraft. I loaded and unloaded baggage.

I thought it was a great place to work. At the time, people who re-tired from Southwest Airlines after twenty or thirty years had sizable retirement accounts, and they could fly any airline for free. The airline industry was famous for major benefits, such as cheap travel and a great retirement.

I started at not much more than minimum wage. At the time, I knew it would take me eighteen years to reach the maximum pay scale.

At first, for about six months, I lived in an apartment with room-mates. After that, I was on my own.

It was while working in San Antonio for Southwest Airlines that I first injured my neck. The injury may *not* have been accidental. Here's what happened:

I was working with a guy who went by the nickname of Bull. He was a heavyset guy, and he was up in the belly of the airplane, loading bags.

Things were going slowly, as they always did with this particular co-worker. "Bull," I said, "you move slower than two turtles fucking."

I crawled up the conveyor belt to help him. When I was entering the bin, the door suddenly came down hard on my neck.

Did Bull pull the latch on me? He denied it, but I had my doubts.

I finally came back to Las Vegas to finish college at the University of Nevada Las Vegas. I might have stayed in San Antonio, but the univer-sity there wouldn't accept many of the credits I had earned in Nevada. I wasn't going to repeat college credits. I took some college courses during my time in San Antonio, but I knew I had to go back to Nevada if I wanted to earn my degree in a reasonable amount of time.

My plan was to get my degree in Nevada and hightail it to San Diego, the most fun location of all the places I had experienced up to that point. There, I would pick up a job in sales.

I finished my business degree from UNLV with an emphasis in mar-keting. But right when I was graduating, I spotted a posting for a loan officer position on a bulletin board at school. The job listing was with a firm called New Century Mortgage.

I pursued that opportunity—*relentlessly*. I had bugged Southwest Air-lines about job openings, and I used the same strategy with New Century.

Bill was the guy doing the interviewing, and I was tireless in my pursuit.

"What's going on with the job?" Over and over, I would call. "What's going on with the job?"

I called. And called.

Someone else at New Century Mortgage noticed my persistence and said to Bill, "Hey, why don't you hire the guy that looks like Chris Farley?" Farley was a comedian with *Saturday Night Live* in the early 1990s. Many people have said I look like a cross between Chris Farley and Quentin Tarantino.

I was breaking my back throwing luggage for Southwest Airlines. It was a blue-collar job, and it hadn't taken me long to realize the physical work would take its toll on my body—and my spirit. I wanted to move up. I wanted to live in a nice house. I wanted to drive a nice car.

My initial idea was to keep my Southwest Airlines job and give away all my shifts so I could keep the benefits. I was never late the whole time I worked there. I called in sick on a very rare occasion.

As a Southwest Airlines ramp agent, you bid your shifts based on seniority. By 1998 when I was graduating college, I had accumulated a lot of seniority. I bid the night shift—overnight mail. That was the shift where you loaded mail onto carts to take to the planes. It was a welcome change of pace from throwing bags. I got rid of all my shifts, with the exception of Friday. My hours were midnight to eight in the morning. I loved it.

I did not work the flight line, which was dangerous. That's where most accidents happen and people get hurt. Overnight mail was a better and safer job than working around passenger jets. Working on a regular flight line is dangerous work. You are around a lot of heavy equipment and marshaling in aircraft. You are always getting blasted by heat from the jet engines and, of course, it's incredibly noisy. You must drive out the planes before they can taxi on their own. You also must chalk the tires when they land and remove them, which is scary as the plane can roll back and take off a foot. With overnight mail, I also did not have to park at the airport. I could clock in at the freight house. In short, overnight mail made my life much easier.

The plan worked perfectly for a year. I had an awesome Southwest Airlines job and was making great money as a loan officer. It was when I got my real estate license at the end of 1999 that things became complicated with Southwest.

When it came to me going after a full-time job with New Century, my persistence finally paid off again. New Century Mortgage offered me a job and two ways to go with my salary: I could choose a small salary with bigger commissions, or I could go with a larger salary with smaller commissions. I took the small salary. The incentives were tantalizing, and I knew I would respond to that kind of motivation.

It worked.

New Century Mortgage was a huge national firm. I became the top producer in Las Vegas, and I was in the top ten every month for six months straight on the national rankings too.

My job was as a loan officer. I gathered all the paperwork and qualified applicants for new mortgages or refinance applications. I checked debt-to-income ratios, verified mortgage histories, checked tax returns. It was all detail work.

New Century Mortgage was a subprime lender, so their rates were high. So were the points they charged up front.

Mortgage loans, however, were widely available. New Century, in fact, would loan money to people who really didn't qualify. (This practice led to the subprime meltdown in 2007 and 2008.) When I saw how generous they were, I figured that the potential pool of customers might be expanded by getting the names of loan applicants who had been *rejected* by other firms, like Bank of America.

While working at New Century Mortgage, I met another loan officer by the name of Mike Gonzales. He sold wholesale paper to the loan offices, who, in turn, sold to the general public. Mike was let go for what the company claimed was lack of performance. In fact, his boss wanted to take over his accounts. It was about money. When he was let go, Mike became my biggest competitor because I got most of my referrals from Bank of America, and he had worked there previously, so he knew all the bankers I was hitting up for referrals.

Mike ended up starting his own mortgage company but lost that business during the financial crisis. In the end, he came to my firm and worked with me for about ten years, beginning in 2008. Later, I would teach him all about commercial real estate.

Mike is short like me. You can't tell him what to do. We ended up becoming good friends until the car wreck.

. . . .

I started nagging Bank of America for all their "turndowns." The branches said I needed permission from Elizabeth, who oversaw lending for the entire state of Nevada. She gave the blessing for me to get the names of the applicants rejected by Bank of America.

So, I started calling people who thought they had been shut out of getting a new mortgage, and I'd say, "Have I got a deal for you."

And then I'd qualify them. Our rate might be higher than the rate from a bank, but it wasn't hard to bring the customers along—to reassure them that the value of their house was bound to go up, that we could find a way to make it all work.

I figured out the game in rapid fashion. It wasn't hard. But after about seven months, I wanted to work with a mortgage banker at regular rates.

I got hired at Greystone Financial Group in 1998, and I worked there until the end of 1999. During all this time, I held down both jobs. One for Southwest Airlines (even though I gave away most of my shifts) and as a loan officer—full-time.

The mortgage banking business was the same kind of hustle, but better, because I could work with other brokers to get good mortgage rates for customers.

. . . .

Allow me a brief side story that shows how trouble kind of knows how to follow me around.

Around this time, I took a trip to San Diego. I always loved the city.

I had gone to boot camp in San Diego, and also lived there part-time during the Gulf War.

I visited my former naval boss, Rob, who had become a hippie at Ocean Beach. He was working as an electrician at Legoland. I had drinks with him and his girlfriend. One evening, they were going out for Valentine's Day as a couple, so I decided to go off alone.

Down to Tijuana.

I should have known better. Ahead was another close call with death.

Tijuana always meant drama—almost every time I had gone there.

I was hanging out at Revolution Street. I had a couple of drinks and was low on money and decided to leave. The problem was I only had five dollars on me. A taxi ride cost six dollars to get back.

An aggressive young taxi person ushered me into his cab. He was athletic-looking and started asking me a lot of questions.

"What do you do for a living?" he asked.

"I throw cargo for a living," I lied. I did not want to tell him I had become a loan officer.

The hairs on the back of my neck were going up.

"I've only got five bucks," I said.

"No problem," he said. He drove me to an ATM. "Get out ten thousand pesos."

The exchange rate was seven pesos to the dollar—about $1,400.

He pulled out a knife. I ran away and crossed a highway, narrowly avoiding getting hit.

I dived behind a bus stop bench and flagged down another taxi. I had just escaped death in Tijuana.

It was the last time I ever went there.

I quit Southwest Airlines at the beginning of the new millennium. It was February 2000. I had six figures in retirement with Southwest Airlines but lost most of it when I invested in dot-com companies during the crash in 2000. I was now destitute and starting real estate. It was either sink or swim. Make it or become homeless!

CHAPTER 6

First Taste of Real Estate

Back in Las Vegas, I was settling into the routines of the working world. In fact, I also took in my first dog, a black Lab named Midnight. She was all black with a white patch on her chest. She was three months old. It was New Year's Eve 1999. Having a dog meant that I wasn't going out—or *staying out*—late. Midnight was always in the back of my mind. I really cared for that dog. I could see my life starting to change in many ways, and they were all good.

Upon graduating college and when I worked as a loan officer, I went to real estate school at night. I was always looking ahead in life, always wanting to make things better for myself.

After graduating from real estate school, I waited two years to take the licensing test. What motivated me to finally sign up for the exam was an exchange with a real estate agent named Dan. He referred a loan to me. *Fine.* Except he was acting very uptight that I would make 2 percent commission from the deal, while he was making 6 percent!

He belittled me. He made me feel like he was much better than I was, and that I didn't deserve my 2 percent. That exchange motivated me to get off my rocking chair and go take the real estate test to get my Nevada real estate license.

Studying was no problem. I had a goal, and I bore down.

On my first crack at the test, I passed. I was good to go.

Through my work in mortgage lending, I had come to know a real estate agent named Beth. She owned a small boutique office with a few dozen agents. Beth worked 100 percent in residential real estate except for two agents—her husband and another guy named Bill, who is still a friend of mine to this day. Those two agents handled the commercial real estate section of Beth's portfolio.

"Hey, I want to be in land," I said to Beth. Over and over. "I want to be your land guy."

No dice.

Beth wouldn't let me switch over to commercial real estate. I left to work for a company called Realty Executives, which gave me more flexibility. It allowed me to run my own business, but I had to pay a fee for every transaction and for rent.

I was stuck in residential, but I was a quick study. I soon realized that signing up a client comes down to one of three options. These three options form the basis of my core philosophy in the real estate game.

First is the easy one. If I hit somebody up to sell a property and they say "yes," I'm done. There's no more selling, on my part. I've got a client.

The second option is an objection. For instance, a potential client wants help selling their property, but they have a price in mind that is completely unrealistic.

"Well," I say, "do you want to price your property to sell, or do you want to price it in fantasyland? Do you really want to sell, or are you just testing the market?"

That's something I can deal with. I can overcome an objection.

What's impossible is the third option. A condition.

If a potential client needs to get approval from a whole team of co-owners before engaging—if no decision can be made without a whole committee's approval—then I'm in an impossible spot. That's a condition. The potential client isn't really in control, and I don't need to waste my time. Most potential large commercial deals involve a conglomerate of owners, and that creates complexity and long discussions. You must win over, occasionally, many more decision-makers. It's a harder game to play.

However, if there is the slightest opportunity for me to represent a client, I'm relentless. I don't take no for an answer. I keep coming up with ideas. I keep showing potential clients how creative I'll be and how hard I'll work once I'm officially their representative. Being timid and shy does not get the job done. It's always good to let potential clients see your commitment and determination.

In a two-year period that ended in the summer of 2002 with Realty Executives, I sold around 100 houses. That's a lot of houses, about five closings per month. I made about six figures every year—a long way from shore patrol in the U.S. Navy and a heck of a lot more than the $6.50 per hour I started at with Southwest Airlines, or even the $10.75 an hour I was making after being there close to seven years.

I was active. I was a top producer. I was a sales guy through and through. I was finding myself and hitting my stride.

At the same time, I knew that residential had its limitations.

I remember one listing I had in Boulder City when I just started my own real estate company, called Realty Specialists. The listing was about twenty-five miles southeast of Downtown Las Vegas on the way to Hoover Dam.

We were on our third or fourth counteroffer. They didn't have a fax machine (this was back before the heavy use of email and electronic signatures, etc.) so each counteroffer required a trip that practically took up the whole day. This was a $130,000 house that would generate a $4,000 commission check.

That's when I said to myself, *no more houses.* Houses are lucrative if you work hard, and that's fine, but the sheer volume was too time-consuming. I was very consistent in my income, but I could also feel the tedium of all the running around. At that time, the average home price was around $150,000.

I opened my company in June 2002. It was called PlanetForSale.com, doing business as Realty Specialists. I rented space from a big land developer named Morgan. Morgan was a big land broker, and I asked him to teach me the land game. Why would he do that? For one simple reason: I offered him half my commissions for two years if he showed me the ropes of commercial real estate.

Morgan was twelve years older than me. I was in my early thirties and Morgan was in his mid-forties.

Commercial real estate is a whole different deal, especially when it comes to selling raw land. An office building is relatively easy. As with residential real estate, the buyer and the seller can check comparable sales, measure the square footage, and come up with a number. You develop what's called a cap rate—a *capitalization* rate. The cap rate is often calculated as the ratio between the net operating income produced by an asset, such as an office building, and the cost to buy it. The cap rate is, essentially, the way to determine market value.

But vacant, raw land is another deal altogether. You've got to look at how the land can be improved to its "highest and best use" under local zoning. The other big question is whether the zoning can be changed. This is where it becomes a cutthroat game.

Let's say a piece of property is zoned for two dwelling units per acre but might have the possibility of being used at fifty dwellings per acre—that would mean a much higher price for the same piece of dirt once the property is zoned and entitled for the new and intended use.

There's another way to play the game too. The following method is not one I liked to play—and didn't play. I had a reputation for representing sellers and working to get them the top price I could find. This next method is legitimate, but I didn't care for it.

Let's say you're buying five acres for $1 million. You go into escrow while you're waiting for the deal to close. You get an appraisal that says the land is worth $15 million. You go get a loan—before the closing— for $10 million. The buyer cashes out $9 million. You could leverage land like that (at least, before the big downturn in 2008). This was done on a grand scale before the financial crisis.

It wasn't all big operators doing this, it was regular people too. Schoolteachers, anybody. Suddenly, they're worth substantial money through leverage.

If you can buy the land for X, but know it can be rezoned for Y, you're in. You bring a piece of property to its higher, better use. Land, in short, is the number one paying job in the world.

Land, in the long run, is always number one.

Dealing drugs, number two. (But I am not a criminal and would never have considered this option, of course.)

Now, let me introduce a complicating factor. At least, a factor that makes the land game even more competitive.

There are four jurisdictions in the Las Vegas Valley. There's the City of Las Vegas, Clark County, Henderson, and North Las Vegas. That means you have four different bureaucracies to deal with in terms of working to improve land to its highest, best use.

In addition to the rezoning tactic, there's another way to make money. Luck.

Or maybe luck *combined* with intuition.

I went into the office one day to do some cold-calling. I found a seller who had property on the southwest corner of Jones and Blue Diamond Road. The property was 2.27 acres altogether. The seller told me that I could buy it for $1.2 million. But as part of the deal, I would have to close escrow in thirty days. He agreed to pay me a 3 percent commission.

I took the deal to my CPA and another former friend, and we all arranged to buy the property together. My CPA came up with the loan amount plus another $200,000 of interest reserves to make payments. The seller told me that there was a "one in a million" chance the government might claim the property through eminent domain.

"But I would not worry about that," he said.

My CPA was concerned, but I told him from what I understood, the government would have to pay us what it was worth. I had a feeling we were purchasing the land at a price well below market value.

We bought the property for the agreed-upon price of $1.2 million. Shortly after we bought the property, we were ordered to sell it to the state for highway improvements that were in the works.

We ended up selling for close to $4 million—not bad for a one-year investment!

In 2006, I was doing very well. I had even purchased a getaway house in downtown Huntington Beach, California.

. . . .

With residential, you can sell over 100 houses in a very short period. You've got a lot of commission checks rolling in. With commercial, you are working on a much longer time horizon—but the payoffs can be huge and much bigger than with a house. There are many real estate agents who can't make the switch from residential to commercial.

You have to believe in yourself. You have to learn to not take no for an answer.

When I started my own company, I did not do strictly commercial. For the first two years, I mixed houses and land. While I was making the transition to 100 percent commercial, I made six figures a year in gross commissions.

When I switched my focus to commercial real estate specializing in land, I was pulling in seven figures a year—after paying Morgan half of my commissions for showing me the ropes. Morgan did very well. In fact, he often flipped out of deals and probably made eight figures off the deal I brokered for him. I gave him half my fees for two years.

In 2006, my friend Mike Kennedy was developing a property near the intersection of West Flamingo Road and Highway 215 in West Las Vegas.

"Hey Mike," he said, "why don't you buy an office building from me?"

Why not? I bought a 2,200-square-foot office condo and moved out of Morgan's office to my own location. I brought in another agent to work for me, and an assistant, too, to help run the office.

Was I doing well?

By any measure, *yes.*

In addition to owning the office building, I had purchased the house in Huntington Beach for getaways. I had a house in West Las Vegas. Not bad for a guy who was throwing bags at the airport five years earlier.

I was also floating around $7-8 million in land debt. People got rich buying and selling land by leveraging and then reselling it for a profit. Things went up in value and never really went down.

Until, one day, they did.

At this point in my career, I was quite pompous. In 2006, I was in my mid-thirties. I was a land guy—selling what I wanted to sell. No houses! I knew I should have settled down and had a family. But I was making serious money and wanted to focus on my career. I also wanted to have fun. I trained in Huntington Beach with a gorgeous trainer named Erin. I'd go out with her and her girlfriends, I would hang out at Perqs Bar and other dive surf bars in the area.

Right before I bought my beach house, I was dating a beautiful girl named Deidra. I met her through some college friends from UNLV. She had red hair and fair skin. She was trim, athletic, had a great figure, and a fiery and outgoing personality. Everybody loved Deidra. We dated off and on from 2002 to 2005.

One time we went out, and we were driving in my car, and she said a guy from her church wanted to marry her. But she told me that she wanted to marry me. She gave me an ultimatum. I needed to make a decision or she would marry this other guy. I blew it. I turned down her proposal. To this day, I'm sad and remorseful about my choice. I was enjoying my lifestyle, and I didn't see the bigger picture, the long-term possibilities of a wife and family. This was a huge mistake. Had I settled down with Deidra, I know for a fact none of the things that happened to me would have occurred; my search for a family would have been resolved, and I wouldn't have succumbed to the temptations that were soon to come my way.

When I went to Huntington Beach, I always drove. It's only about a five-hour drive from Las Vegas, and I always took my Labradors with me. By then, I had adopted a yellow Lab, a rescue named Laurel, in addition to the black Lab named Midnight I already had. I enjoyed the beach by day and all the bars were right in my backyard.

It wasn't as if I thought I was better than anyone else, but I knew I had more *belief* in myself than others had in their own selves. I knew then that the secret to success in life starts with one simple concept.

Believe in yourself.

This was in the years leading up to the Great Recession, which really hit hard beginning in 2008. I had invested occasionally in real estate syndicates through my friend Morgan and several others. But then Morgan made decisions on his partnerships that were not in favor of his investors. He would put debt on the partnerships, and eventually, he lost all his partnerships to foreclosures.

He lost a bunch of my money. I didn't believe in that type of behavior. I lost around a hundred grand. Not the worst, but still. Who wants to lose that much money?

What I realized about most developers raising money on their partnerships is they are all about themselves, and not the investors. It's the old saying, *getting rich on other people's money*. That is what they do. Developers live in multimillion-dollar homes based on the hard-earned dollars of their investors.

· · · ·

The year before the big crash, I was doing very well. The leverage started catching up with all the other investors. When people were starting to struggle to make money, I made close to seven figures in gross commissions—from about a dozen real estate transactions and around $45 million to $50 million in total sales in 2007.

This was down from 2004 and 2005 when I was making double that amount. In 2006, my income was down substantially, but I knew it was because I was hanging around my beach house too much, having fun.

That's the deal with commercial real estate: no house tours. Very few showings. Of course, you walk a property and tour buildings, but there are far fewer appointments with much less chauffeuring of buyers. The point is, you can be on the beach and take a phone call. My income might have been down, but it was still good.

In commercial real estate, the people you're working with are all familiar with the process and how it works. For the most part, you're dealing with a more sophisticated clientele. They're *experienced*.

The big problem in 2007—and the next year, too, when things went completely south in 2008—was the banks. In their infinite wisdom, the banks allowed leverage on the properties. As in, *too much* leverage.

In 2007, I started working in industrial warehouses. I listed the corner at Harmon and Valley View and co-brokered it with my now good friend Danielle Steffen. It was around 40,000 square feet, and I sold it for almost $8 million. I had my first taste of something in commercial other than land. I found my secondary discipline.

It was Danielle who may have possibly saved my life in 2007 from someone who was being investigated for the disappearance of several people. I was working on a for sale-by-owner (FSBO) warehouse near Dean Martin Drive, and I was trying to get the listing. The owner's name was David Dale Morgan. I toured the property and met with the owner. He did not want to list, but I relentlessly pursued him. He specifically told me he did not want me contacting him for a listing. I did anyway.

That is what I do, and that is who I am!

I called him all the time. One day, David Dale Morgan called me back.

"Hey, Michael," he said. "I want to buy some land in Mesquite, and I want you to represent me and show me the property.

I was very excited about this. Around this time, I talked to my new friend Danielle, that I co-brokered the warehouse with, and told her about winning this person over. She immediately told me that David Dale Morgan is on the news, and he is being investigated for the murder of his wife's lover and the disappearance of 3 others.

Yikes, I was stunned. I pulled up the news, and she was right. I remember him becoming really upset because I was relentlessly pursuing him, and then I remembered when he snapped and became nice.

I felt a tingle on the back of my neck. I called David and told him I could not go to Mesquite with him, and then, boom, the very next day he's arrested and being featured on the news. David Dale Morgan was under house arrest for many years. He died on November 11, 2018. His obituary has a comment which reads, verbatim:

"David was real man, loved beating women, scaring his own kids and killing people. and was always up for a little bullying. Suspected Fed rat and I would have done something about the guy myself but they would have known. Rest in peace Dina Lee. I love you, Dino."

My friend had saved me. I will always love her for that.

. . . .

The big problem with the financial crisis had to do with buyers putting land in escrow, turning around and getting a loan from a bank for more money than they were in escrow for, and cashing out large sums. For example, $500,000 or $1 million—with no skin in the game. I would even see this played on a grander scale in the tens of million range.

But the collateral wasn't there. The banks made loans too easy. Appraisers helped, inflating the alleged value of what a property might earn.

When the banks started failing in 2008—particularly when the vaunted Lehman Brothers collapsed in September—it was the beginning of the end. So much land had been leveraged to the hilt. Prices on raw land in the Valley dropped 95 percent. The game was over.

But every market crash is an opportunity, right? Sell at the wedding and buy at the funeral—that's the old maxim.

I had never been able to buy land without partners, but that changed when the prices crashed. I knew it would be a long recovery. You don't go through such a cataclysmic crash and immediately bounce back. When the prices dropped, I knew they would remain bargain deals for many years.

I went out and purchased three pieces of land for myself. These purchases were without any partners. Years later, when the market turned back up, I sold those parcels of land for a substantial profit.

I managed my way through the Great Recession. I kept my eyes open, paid attention to the market. I looked for opportunity. Many other brokers got wiped out. But I was still standing, and eager to keep my business rolling, when all the dust had cleared.

. . . .

The one thing that occurred to me from time to time was that I should be married, that I should be starting a family. There seemed to be a big hole in my life—something missing.

In December 2011, I was given a very clear picture of this fact.

That year, I was down in San Antonio for my brother's wedding. The first night in town, my brother had a nervous breakdown, and he violently assaulted me. Without going into the details, I refrained from ever striking back. How would it look if my brother was all bruised before his wedding and was the result of me striking him? A profound voice popped into my head: he was doing this because you told him you were going to leave him your money. It was not something I thought, it was another entity altogether that said this. I could tell that voice in my head did not come from my own consciousness. I was startled when this thought popped into my head. I begged my mom to get him off of me, but she just sat there with a smirk on her lips. My brother tried to apologize after the assault happened, but I refused his apology and left my mom's house.

The next day my mom called me up and begged me not to be the best man at my brother's wedding. I went down and was going to accept my brother's apology. My brother said something bizarre. He said he remembered it as me attacking him. Unbeknownst to me, he lied to his future wife's family about what happened and told them I assaulted him. Later at his wedding, I felt fear for my life. While I was having dinner, I looked over my shoulder and saw a guy with a gun glaring at me. Out of all the people at the wedding, I was the only one he was staring at. When I stared at him, he quickly looked away. I went back to eating, then quickly whipped my head around, and he was staring at me again.

I thought I must be crazy. A few minutes later, my sister Mary said the guy was there to shoot me if I got out of line. I was deeply hurt; I was the best man and treated in a horrific fashion, not just from the assault, but also at the wedding where I was to be an honored guest.

That first night after my brother assaulted me, I left my mom's house and prayed. I prayed for my own heir. What is success and money if you have no one to enjoy it with or leave it to? I did not want to leave it to my brother anymore after what happened.

During my prayer, a tingling sensation came over me.

About an hour after praying, I was hanging out with a girlfriend from my high school days. Her name was Chrissy.

"Hey, I'm friends with Teresa on Facebook," said Chrissy.

Teresa was a girl I'd had a one-night stand with when I was home on leave from the Navy twenty-one years earlier. Why would Chrissy bring up Teresa?

Teresa was four or five years older than me. Back during my high school days, Teresa would buy beer for me and my friends. We were too young for the liquor stores, but Teresa didn't mind helping us out.

Teresa had joked with me when I joined the Navy on my deferred enlistment program. "Mike, be careful," she had said. "I have a thing for sailors."

Sure enough, when I came home on leave in December of 1989, we had that one-night fling.

It wasn't the first. We'd had another one before I joined the Navy, right after I had turned 18. We were at a high school party and went to one of the guest bedrooms.

Bringing up her name brought it all back.

"Great," I said to Chrissy. "I'm glad you're in touch with Teresa. So?"

"Did you know she has a daughter who looks just like you?" said Chrissy.

The daughter's name was Tina. Her birth name was Christina. I took one look at the photo, and I knew. There was no question. There was no need for a DNA test as far as I was concerned. However, Tina later insisted on one and sure enough, I was her father.

I was amazed. On the night I had prayed for a family—I discovered I had one. It was an overwhelming and powerfully emotional moment. *I had been a father for twenty-one years!*

However, the relationship wasn't as close as I wanted it to be. That would be asking too much, to expect Tina to make room for me. I realized how awkward it was for her, to suddenly meet her biological father. To this day, I have nothing but affection and love for Tina.

She was on a Christian missionary trip in England when I first reached out to her. On that trip she met a guy from Paris, and she really thought he was "the one." After coming back to the United States, she saved up money to go see him. Tina was very eager to pursue the relationship. I stepped in and paid for the flight. I wanted to support her. She flew back to Europe, but the Paris guy didn't pan out.

She came home and quickly met another guy, got married, and soon had a child of her own.

Brianna was born on June 24, 2018. Brianna's birth made me a grandfather.

I like to think that if I hadn't helped get Tina to France, she'd still be pining for the guy in Paris. In other words, I'd like to think I helped her find her husband more quickly. That's how intertwined we all are in this life. It's crazy.

I bought Tina a new car. I showered her with money for a while up until I paid for her trip to France. I had always wanted someone to love and share my success with. I realized through age and wisdom that if you are successful and have no one to share your success with, it means nothing in life.

The startling addition of a daughter in my life was a welcome development. But deep down, I was still missing that complete feeling of family and family connections. After all, I had not been around Tina at all during her youth and formative years. My closest family connection was my grandma, whom I would talk to on a regular basis. As much as I love Tina, I didn't raise her. She didn't live with me, not even in the same state. The connection was as good as I could hope for given the circumstances, but there was still a gap in my life.

I love Tina and my granddaughter very much. Tina's adoptive parents were the uncle and aunt of her half-brother, whom they had adopted several years before Tina was born. The fact that Tina would grow up with her biological brother brought me joy. She is one of the greatest of daughters on this earth! She never once asked me for a penny. I did these things for her because I love her.

Maybe that yearning for a real family, one that truly supported me, played a role in what happened toward the end of 2012.

I'm not sure. I will likely never know.

At the end of 2012, a new prospect landed on my doorstep. This prospect had the potential to clinch my status as one of the top commercial land brokers in all of Las Vegas. It went hand in hand with another long-term opportunity that, at that point, I had been pursuing for nine years.

Together, these two monster opportunities were the equivalent of having a double rainbow—and both rainbows ending in gigantic pots of gold.

The 2012 opportunity began with a mailer.

One of the routine things I did as a land broker was to send out mailers to people who owned land. It's a simple marketing tool—easy and cheap to do. The mailers say, "I may have a buyer for you. If you're interested in selling, call me." The mailers are prospecting for clients.

It works! People do call. They're curious. And remember, this was when we were just starting to come off the long downturn from the years-long recession. Owners who had been sitting on property, hoping for a comeback, were interested to see what kind of prices we might be able to bring them.

Suddenly, the sellers were waking up. Las Vegas, as a soon-to-be booming city, was coming back to life.

CHAPTER 7

A Perfect Weapon

I realized when I was in kindergarten that I was one of the smallest people in my class. As a military family, we moved a lot. Not only was it hard to make new friends, but my size intimidated no one—except me. It was like I had a target on my back, and I was bullied from a young age.

Martial arts became a calling that eventually led me to escape certain death. Maybe if I hadn't been bullied, I wouldn't have had a fixation with martial arts. Who knows?

As a kid, I constantly nagged my parents to get me into a martial art class. They always refused. It was when we moved from Homestead, Florida to Prattville, Alabama, that I finally got my way.

In ninth and tenth grade, I took tang soo do—a Korean-based and karate-based martial art, the same style Chuck Norris studied. Later, in my mid-twenties when I moved back to San Antonio and worked for Southwest Airlines, I started taking kenseido, which had elements of aikido, karate, wing chun, kung fu, and northern Chinese martial arts.

In 2010, I felt a desire to start taking martial arts again. When I was living in Las Vegas, there was a dojo across the street from my real estate office. It was run by Jeff Speakman, the star of an action movie called *The Perfect Weapon* that came out in 1991. Speakman was an A-list movie star. His style of fighting was kenpo karate. His instructor was Ed Parker, who taught Elvis Presley, and who was also trained with Bruce Lee.

That October, I started taking private lessons. I went to some group classes, too, but the evening hours for the group work didn't suit my schedule. I found that I couldn't go to sleep after an evening class. My head would be too busy reviewing all the karate moves. I preferred training during the middle of the day. With my real estate company right across the street, I could always go during lunchtime or whenever I got the chance. It was perfect.

I worked directly with Speakman, the main master. He was a specialist in the art of American kenpo and Japanese gōjū-ryū, which translates to "hard-soft style." He had earned black belts in each, a rare feat, and had franchises all over the world. I wasn't the most popular martial artist at the dojo because I had so much direct instruction from the master himself. I would sometimes correct other black belts when they were demonstrating technique. When I noticed they were doing something not in the way Speakman taught it, I would speak up.

"Mr. Speakman teaches the technique this way," I'd say.

(Martial arts masters are always addressed as "Mr." as a sign of great respect.)

The look I would get from the other black belts when I spoke up was one of death. If looks could kill, I would have been a dead man back then.

Even in a dojo, jealousy is a thing.

Mr. Speakman would not let his students spar while achieving the first two belts—going from white to yellow and then from yellow to orange. He wanted to spend that first year making sure you could maintain a 50/50 weight distribution and would not topple over from being off balance in a fight. He also used this time to make sure you perfected your kicks and strikes.

In January 2012, I had to spar for my purple belt. My office assistant at the time, Jennifer, and her husband Dean, had begun taking kenpo karate with Mr. Speakman six months before me. In fact, listening to Jennifer talk about their experience had motivated me to take more classes.

When my test was coming up to move from orange to purple belt, Jennifer started taunting me that I might have to fight her husband, who was one level above me. And if I did have to fight him, she claimed he would kick my ass.

I said, "Really?"

I knew that whatever happened in life, I could not let her husband kick my ass. How would that make me look to my assistant?

Sure enough, when testing for my purple belt, Mr. Speakman called on both of us to spar.

Game on!

I realized how little impact his kicks and punches were having on me. I ended up clinching with him, and then I kicked him in the groin multiple times. Next, I threw him on the ground. I did not know how to fight on the ground, and he swept me up and then ended up on top of me. I mule-kicked his chest so hard he must have flown at least five feet in the air before landing on the ground.

On *his* ass.

We started striking again, and immediately, I got him in the clinch again. There was a yell for "Break!"

But I could not resist. A second after the yell, I threw him many feet in the air. Once again, and for the third time in that fight, he ended up on his ass.

Mr. Speakman gave me tremendous shit, through text messages, because I'd thrown Dean after he yelled "Break."

My assistant Jennifer was amazed when I saw her the following Monday. I told her I did not mean anything by it. It was a belt test with Mr. Speakman, and I felt as if I had to make a good impression.

Dean showed up at my office later that same Monday. He complained that he was super sore, especially where I kicked him. I felt bad about this.

Shortly after the Dean fight, I was sparring, and the fight went to the ground. It was a noon class. Judd, who had been a spectator when I tested for the purple belt against Dean, was running the class. Judd wanted to make the class about sparring. In fact, this was going to be my first official sparring class. I was nervous about this as I'd already tested and didn't want to tempt fate.

Right before sparring, I was talking to this big black guy by the name of Andre.

"Andre, how much do you lift?" I asked.

Andre was a skilled martial artist. He was muscular and much larger than me.

"Oh," said Andre. "I don't lift weights anymore ever since I had my arm snapped in jiu-jitsu."

That sounded awful. And painful. "I hope I never get my arm snapped," I replied.

Judd overheard this exchange.

With more than a little fear and worrying about what Judd might be thinking as he stood across from me on the mat, I started sparring with my instructor.

I went to the ground, and before I knew it, his legs were wrapped around my head, squeezing my left jaw. He had put me in something called an arm bar.

An arm bar is designed to force an opponent to submit. It's a very common move in judo and jiu-jitsu as these are the common "grappling" arts, although it can be applied to any martial art where ground-work (fighting while not standing) is needed.

Just as it sounds like it might do, the move puts tremendous pressure on the arm. In combat situations, the move is designed to break an arm. When I was being submitted in training, no one had ever told me that to stop, all I had to do was slap the mat or the opponent.

I did neither.

I did not even know what "tapping out" meant. I was desperately trying to free my arm, which exacerbated the situation.

I heard a very loud snap, and immediately thought, "All right, these guys really don't like me." It was all those private lessons with Jeff Speakman. They were bullying me. The instructor was bullying me.

Judd burst out laughing.

"Let me get you an ice pack," he said.

I was horrified. Did this guy just snap my left arm on purpose?

It was a very humbling experience, particularly because Judd was smaller than me. It taught me right then and there that size is not as important in a fight as technique and the spirit of the individual.

Toward the end of 2012, I tested for my green belt. This belt was a big deal as it was the belt right before brown belt. At the brown belt level, you wear a black gee, the traditional karate uniform, and you become a teacher.

Every year, Mr. Speakman holds a camp in Las Vegas. It's an opportunity to earn your brown belt or higher. At the end, you're required to spar. I wanted to go from green belt to brown belt. All the green belts and brown belts are supposed to spar with each other. Same for the black belts.

Right after becoming a green belt and about seven months before heading to this camp, which was very important to me, a woman named Kathy Little made this comment that really stuck with me: "Mike, you're going to have to spar at camp."

She said it in a very ominous way. In fact, I felt that sense of paralyzing fear. I would find out later that my intuition was both powerful and a gift.

I couldn't figure out why she would single me out of a class of thirty students. She would only say this to me, and she said it in a very taunting way. *Everybody* was going to have to spar at camp. Why me? Why single me out? I knew something was going to happen.

One option was to skip the camp. I could simply forgo the whole trip. Or I could take care of business. It was a pivotal moment.

I felt if I avoided going to camp, I would have been a coward in the eyes of all the students. I decided to take care of business, to face whatever was to come. But I didn't want to show up unprepared. I started doing all sorts of research online.

I was driven by one question: who would be the best person to secretly train with and learn the art of ground fighting?

My martial arts skills were sorely lacking when it came to ground fighting. Las Vegas was the home of the UFC, Ultimate Fighting Championship. I knew of somewhere I could secretly train like Batman and take care of business.

I came across a video of Robert Drysdale training with Forest Griffith. Drysdale was a multi-world champion in jiu-jitsu. He was also an undefeated MMA fighter, known for winning all his fights within seconds in mixed martial arts, sometimes known as cage fighting. I knew another of his champions was Frank Amir, and he was also Randy Couture's jiu-jitsu coach.

Secretly, I started training with Robert Drysdale. It was very intimidating at first. The people at his dojo did not even have much left of their ears. I would wonder how many battles they endured to achieve such badges of glory. Jiu-jitsu practitioners would consider the scarring of their ears as points of pride.

During this time, one of the professional fighters saw me having a private session with Robert Drysdale and asked if I wanted to learn the art of Thai boxing. Sure, I thought, what a great weapon to have in case the Kenpo Black Belt Council really did have something planned for me at the camp.

My new teacher for Thai boxing was James McSweeney, a.k.a. The Sledgehammer. McSweeney was no slouch. He had moved to Thailand at age 15 to train full-time in muay Thai—a form of boxing that includes fists, elbows, shins, and knees. McSweeney was an accomplished kickboxer and had won numerous British, European, and World titles. McSweeney taught me the art of Thai boxing, and I learned the art of taking down larger opponents while also learning the basics of ground fighting from Robert Drysdale. Two masters at their craft.

I devoted four to five hours a day to intense training. Life is a numbers game—whether it's making money in real estate or being an incredible martial artist, you must put in the time.

About a month before the fight at The Orleans Casino, I was incredibly cocky. I was making good money in real estate, and I really thought I had a perfect life. One day in April 2013, I was grappling with a guy who worked as head of security at the Encore Beach Club. He was close to becoming a purple belt, and when I trained with Robert Drysdale, he would pull students to have me fight in front of him. This security guy kneed me hard in the left side of my jaw while I was on the ground breaking his guard. He kneed me so hard that he broke and unhinged my jaw. People would always go 100 percent in front of Robert to get another stripe on their belt—so they could test for the next belt.

This time, I was the victim.

It was painful. There was a sharp, stinging pain like I have never felt before. Robert had me fight through the pain. I decided not to go to the doctor. I thought, *you know what? I'm just going to wear a big head shield when I go to the camp. I won't worry about my jaw.*

My jaw was hurting constantly, but I also knew that if my jaw was broken, I would not be able to test for my brown belt. I'd spent too much time training for this event. I was determined to not give up. Going to the doctor was not an option. I had put in hard work to get my brown belt in kenpo.

Years later, not seeking medical help would prove to be a good thing. Long after the car wreck, when things got complicated with lawsuits and insurance claims, I was asked why I hadn't sought medical help right away.

"How could you have been that hurt if you didn't go to the doctor?" was the standard question from lawyers and insurance agents after the wreck.

"Well, look at my broken, unhinged jaw. I waited a year and a half to get treatment for that," I would say.

After I first got kneed in the jaw, I knew that if I went to the doctor, they would wire my mouth shut for a year—and I wouldn't be able to make a living if I couldn't talk.

So, I went to The Orleans Casino in May 2013. I did all the katas, or forms, and techniques that are required. The sparring and fighting take place toward the end of camp.

All the green and brown belts teamed up.

Me? Not yet.

This went on for a substantial period. There was no partner for me.

Soon, everyone had sparred except for me.

"Sorry," the Black Belt Council said, "you're going to have to fight a black belt."

Not only was the guy they wanted me to fight a black belt—this person appeared ten years younger than me, six inches taller, and 150 pounds heavier. His name was Mike Gorilla.

I had one thought: *Holy smokes.*

He's one of those fighters who could throw a punch—and hit you—from across the room.

But I had all that training with Robert Drysdale and The Sledgehammer (James McSweeney). I also had all my years of private lessons with Mr. Speakman. I knew I would put it to use.

With my broken, unhinged jaw, I was having a bad day.

The colossal giant threw a jab and then a cross. I could not get near this guy to punch back, so I roundhouse-kicked him *hard*. Not at his ribs, but *through* his ribs. I could see his eyes tear up in pain. His face contorted in anger, and he charged me.

He came down on me and put me into a childhood headlock. My headpiece flew off. He tried to knee my broken jaw. I blocked his blow with my forearms.

"Do that again," I thought to myself.

He did it again.

I swept his foot when his other one was trying to knee me in the face. He fell, and he fell hard because of his gargantuan size. Now I was on top of him, grappling him. I had finished seven months of training with the number one ground fighter in the world. I dug my elbow into his trachea and started choking him. I could tell that everybody was in shock at the fact that I had gained advantage on this monster fighter while I was just a lowly green belt who was a fraction of his size. The choke is not the most legal move in the world—but neither was kneeing me in the face while he had me in a childhood headlock.

They broke up the fight.

Jeff Speakman said, "Holy shit, Mike. The Black Belt Council called you out, and you took care of the business."

And Benny the Jet Urquidez—another world-class fighter—stood up with his eyes wide. He gave me two thumbs up.

I heard when they went back to discuss all the people who tested all over the world that my fight was the one everyone was talking about.

Mr. Speakman came up to me after my fight and told me he had never seen anyone fight with such intelligence.

I was grinning from ear to ear. Later, I told Mr. Speakman how I did it—about my secret training. He told me I had been dabbling in the dark side of the force. I loved it! It felt like I was in a "Karate Kid" movie.

It suddenly dawned on me what had happened. "Holy shit," I thought. "I'm a *professional*. Look what I went through. I am a true mixed martial artist!"

My jaw still stung. I would take ibuprofen before going to bed to get rid of it, but I'd still wake up at 2:00 a.m., that stinging sensation preventing me from getting back to sleep.

Because of my jaw, I drifted in and out of martial arts. I ended up taking some serious time off.

About two years later, in the summer of 2015, about six months before the wreck in the shopping center parking lot when I died, I went to see a jaw specialist named Dr. Mark Glyman to see what could be done. He couldn't believe I had been living with the pain for two years.

"Mike, if you had come to me right away after it happened, I would have wired your jaw shut for a year," he said.

"Exactly," I said. "That's why I didn't see you. I needed to keep working."

He made me a special mouthguard to keep my jaw in place, to pop it back in the right position.

But there was still a minor sting, and I was getting very tired of it. The mouth guard worked somewhat, but it was getting hung up on my jawbone and not popping back into place all the way.

In September 2015, five months before the wreck, I broke down. I prayed. It was something I did not do often. Before the wreck, this was a rare occurrence.

"God," I said. "I want you to fix my broken jaw."

It was the worst prayer on the planet—to be that specific and to be thinking only of myself! But I was desperate. I didn't care.

"God, I don't know how you are going to fix my jaw, but if you can't fix it, just let me drop dead of a heart attack by the time I'm fifty-eight."

Immediately after that prayer, however, Robert Drysdale texted me.

"Mike," said the text. "You've got to get in here tomorrow to train."

At that point, I had not trained in over a year. After going to The Orleans Casino to get my brown belt in kenpo karate, I had slacked off. But my prayer had opened me up to the universe. I figured the universe was reaching back out to me.

I went in the next morning at 10:00 a.m. to train. I started grappling with this 17-year-old by the name of Wolfie. He immediately got me in a right arm bar. His legs wrapped around the right side of my jaw. When he applied pressure, there was a loud snap. I immediately tapped out and opened my mouth.

He had popped my jaw back into place.

I thought, *this is weird*. How crazy was it that my jaw was unhinged and dislocated from jiu-jitsu and now gets popped back into place— *from jiu-jitsu?*

That's exactly when Robert Drysdale walked into his dojo, right when my jaw popped back into place. Drysdale pulled me to the side and said something unexpected.

"Mike, I want you to get your blue belt," he said. "I want to make your neck indestructible. I notice you always tap out when others get you in a chokehold. I want you to do these neck crunches every night."

A powerful sensation overcame me when he talked about these neck crunches. Something told me *you better listen to this guy*. It felt that what he was telling me was a matter of life and death. It was as if the entire universe was screaming at me in this moment. Why do I need to make my neck indestructible, what was in store for me in the martial arts community?

I ran into Kathy Little, of all places, at Drysdale Jiu-Jitsu. Kathy was one of the highest-ranking black belts with Jeff Speakman's

Kenpo 5.0 fighting system. Now she and others in Mr. Speakman's fighting system were learning the art of ground fighting—like me! It was like I had left a lasting impression on the Kenpo 5.0 Black Belt Council.

My big mouth, however, got me in trouble again. When I was in a Drysdale class and I saw Kathy, I would tell my friend Harvey and a few others how the Kenpo 5.0 Black Belt Council called me out and how I had to take care of business and had to kick some serious ass.

I could see the steam coming out of Kathy's ears. I knew I was instigating something.

But what?

Sure enough, shortly after all my trash talk, the MMA champion in France, also a student of Jeff Speakman's and Robert Drysdale's, came down to live with Kathy. He was about half my age and a lifelong martial artist. When I did my Thai boxing with a jiu-jitsu and Thai boxing champion by the name of Marcello Nunes, he would record me striking.

It was unnerving to say the least.

What do you think I did? I complained to Jeff Speakman and told him this all started when Judd snapped my arm, and then I talked shit, and then the Black Belt Council called me out.

Jeff Speakman was no dummy. He asked me if I instigated anything recently with Kathy. He kept pushing me.

I could not lie. I admitted that I told everyone at Drysdale Jiu-Jitsu about the beat-down I had to give to Mike Gorilla. I also told him that when I ran into Kathy and Pia for the first time in a couple of years, I had talked shit about Judd snapping my arm. (Pia was a nurse, around 50 years old, who was training with Mr. Speakman in Kenpo 5.0. Pia eventually started training at Drysdale Jiu-Jitsu, and she became a world champion in jiu-jitsu when she was only a blue belt in her age and belt class.)

Pia did so well that Robert Drysdale told me he immediately promoted her to a purple belt. Mr. Speakman gave me so much crap for my trash talk. But I kept training for my blue belt in jiu-jitsu. And, at the same time, I was training to earn more stripes on my brown belt in kenpo so I could eventually get my black belt.

But the main point is that I worked on my neck. Every single night. Hundreds of times. I'd lie on my back with my head elevated. Over and over. My neck became a bulldog neck. When people tried to choke me out during a match, it was no longer a problem. My neck was so strong I could flick attackers away. Opponents' biceps popped off my neck like rubber bands snapping.

Had I not gone back to jiu-jitsu, I would never have worked on my neck. And if my neck wasn't strong that morning in the shopping center parking lot, I wouldn't have survived the wreck. Also, if I did not have this friendly rivalry with Kathy Little, I would not be here now writing this story. Kathy Little unfortunately passed away from an infection while battling breast cancer November 26, 2023. The world lost a great mixed martial artist and a beautiful human being when Kathy left the earth.

The other reason my neck was so powerful was all thanks to Robert Drysdale and Jeff Speakman, who starred in the famous 1991 movie *The Perfect Weapon*. The movie that made Speakman an A-list star.

That day when people tried to murder me, I was the perfect weapon.

During all of this, God was getting ready to save me.

My jiu-jitsu belt test was scheduled for Saturday, February 13, 2016.

The car wreck happened on Wednesday, February 10, 2016.

CHAPTER 8

Big Potential No. 1: The Pig Farm

As I have mentioned, all major landowners were strapped for cash after the financial crisis started to ease in 2012. Landowners could no longer pull loans from their parcels of land anytime they wanted—at least not without banks going over their income with a magnifying glass.

And then for me, in 2012, the tide started to turn.

Suddenly, I had a new opportunity that led me to a man named Farbod Sattari.

Soon thereafter, another longstanding relationship I had been developing since around 2003 seemed like it might be finally ready to pay off too—a well-known pig farm and its well-known owner, my former friend Bob Combs.

Let's start in chronological order, with the pig farm.

PIG FARMS AND RESIDENTIAL REAL ESTATE DON'T MIX

While opportunities were starting to gel with Farbod Sattari, another opportunity was waiting in the wings. I'd been nurturing this one for a long, long time.

Bob Combs owned a legendary, stinky, giant pig farm in the middle of North Las Vegas. The pig farm sat near the community of Eldorado, where my parents had moved years earlier. The city had expanded out to the pig farm. The pig farm composed a small portion of approximately 164-acres of land Bob owned. Who wanted the pig farm as a neighbor? Everyone forever and a day, had wanted the pigs gone. The real estate developers, of course, could imagine how they could build housing and convert the farm to profit.

The farm was one of the most sought-after prizes for residential developers.

But there sat the pig farm, sending out awful aromas over the community. If you lived there, you cared very much about which way the wind was blowing.

Everyone wanted to get rid of the pigs. And I wanted to be the broker on the deal when that happened. How famous would that make me if I was the one to make everyone's lives better? I would become a legend forever in the Valley. This would be talked about long after I left this earth.

Many of my competitors had pursued Bob Combs. One idea was to put a deal with him in escrow, and then go find a real buyer and make millions of dollars in assignment fees. I never practiced that aspect of real estate. Why? Because it did not benefit my clients. If there are millions of dollars to make on a parcel of land, the profit should go to the landowner and not some greedy land broker trying to make the deal all about themselves.

My approach was more genuine, more legit. I wanted to represent him, find him a buyer, and do the best job possible on behalf of Bob Combs. I believed we had a good relationship, and I would be the one he trusted.

I remember when I won Bob Combs over. It was 2004. Beazer Homes developed some acreage next door to the pig farm, and everyone was complaining to the Southern Nevada Health District about the smell.

If you were a guy like Bob Combs with a big parcel that could be developed into profitable real estate, you heard lots of proposals and ideas about how much it was worth and when would be the right time to sell. On the other hand, if you were a guy like Bob Combs sitting on a parcel of land that also generated lots of complaints, you heard your share of whining.

One day I was at Bob's house.

Bob was really upset with all the people who were complaining about him.

"Bob," I said, "*fuck them*. You have lived here for much longer than those people in those new houses. They don't have a right to complain. You were here first. If they didn't like the farm, they shouldn't have bought next door."

His eyes lit up.

He grinned from ear to ear. He liked how I stood up for him when everyone was fighting for him to leave. What I was expressing was common sense. It was also the way I honestly felt. The farm had been around since the 1950s. It was like buying a house next to an airport and then complaining about the jet noise!

One other thing to keep in mind: Bob Combs had a big advantage in terms of expenses. The farm was a lucrative business because of all the free food he received from the casinos. One news report about Combs' approach on this said the Las Vegas buffets generate one pound of food waste per day for every single tourist coming through a casino. That's a lot of food. Combs, whose father purchased the farm in 1963, came up with the idea of using the casino's excess "scraps," and he developed a whole system of cooking them into a slurry that the pigs loved to eat from the troughs. For years, Combs never had to buy his pigs any food. That's a huge way to cut your costs!

Years later during the dark pandemic of 2020, I learned that the farm was struggling. The farm's food supply had dried up because the casinos were shut down, which of course meant all the casino restaurants were closed as well, and that meant no wasted food.

Let's go back now and introduce the other major players in my life and death.

The Sattari family.

CHAPTER 9

Big Potential No. 2: Farbod

Buyers might have been strapped for cash as the nation pulled itself out of the Great Recession, but sellers were occasionally still eager to see if their land holdings could be liquidated.

One guy who called our office identified himself as the owner of Omega Family Limited Partnership. He said his name was Farbod Sattari. He mentioned to my assistant Jennifer that he had four parcels of land to sell. Together, the parcels comprised a 20-acre assemblage near the intersection of Hualapai and Farm in the northwest. The acreage was sizable, of course, and the location was excellent.

Farbod Sattari was curious what my thoughts might be about the prospect of selling it.

Jennifer gathered all the details she could and, being a self-starter and curious to gather more information about the caller, looked up Omega Family Limited Partnership.

"Hey Mike," she said. "You should check this out, this guy has got a huge portfolio of vacant land."

It was staggering how much land was in Omega's name. As long as I had been around the Las Vegas real estate and land brokering scene, I rarely had a client with this type of portfolio. Yes, major home builders held large parcels, but I'd rarely seen anything like this.

I realized I should have known about this major landowner, but I was so busy with people pursuing me to be their broker that I did not analyze every lead that came my way. I looked up the twenty acres near Hualapai and Farm and realized the opportunity that Omega represented.

I made the phone call.

A man with a deep, accented voice answered. It was Farbod Sattari.

Farbod told me that he first reached out to me from one of my mailers in 2005 but that I had not called him back. I vaguely remembered. I also vaguely remembered someone yelling at me. He knew my name, but I had not known his.

In the years to come, the name Farbod Sattari would mean many things to me, from the highest highs to the lowest lows.

I would become intertwined—deeply intertwined—with this guy, his wife, his son, and his daughter. I spent so much time with the entire family that I felt, frankly, like I finally belonged to a family. A powerful and influential Persian family with powerful friends.

Farbod told me he was Italian. Looking back, he was making fun of my Sicilian last name. It took me a couple of months to realize he was from Iran and not Italy. I never made it a habit to lie to people, so when he told me that he was from Italy, I accepted it and never questioned it.

When I realized the extent of Farbod Sattari's real estate holdings, I started pursuing him.

Relentlessly.

I wanted to be his broker. I didn't want a piece here or a scrap there— I wanted to broker his entire portfolio.

I needed to figure out a way to win him over.

But Farbod Sattari proved to be dodgy.

I set up a meeting with a representative from one of the biggest home builders around, KB Home. I brought in one of their top people, Elizabeth Parker. At the time, she was their local Director of Land Acquisition and Strategic Planning. We met in a place perfectly suited for a major land transaction: the Einstein Bros. Bagels at Flamingo Road and Rainbow Boulevard.

Thankfully, Farbod didn't hold it against me that I had not returned his call from eight years earlier. In fact, we hit it off. Farbod was in his mid-sixties. I was 42. He was an Iranian immigrant that became a US citizen, and I liked him immediately. And I could tell he took a liking to me.

I was thrilled to be sitting with Farbod Sattari and Elizabeth Parker. Elizabeth was a big deal. An article in the *Las Vegas Review-Journal* around this time quoted her. She had been speaking at a monthly Southern Nevada Home Builders Association meeting.

"We need to make up for lost time," Parker was quoted as saying. "We want to be able to continue, not only at the rate we're going today, but to grow. We're being very aggressive to maintain our position in the market."

It was clear that money, which had long been on ice, was coming out to play. As a country, we were moving out of the recession. As a city, too, Las Vegas was starting to see optimism return. The term "investment" was no longer a dirty word.

Large tracts of vacant land, like the land that Farbod Sattari owned, were few and far between. Before the recession, 10-acre tracts or more were becoming scarce. And here was a 20-acre gem.

When land is in short supply, prices jump to astronomical numbers. Ten acres is what a single-family developer usually needs, at a minimum, to have a potential development make economic sense. The fewer possible lots you can place on a vacant parcel—lots for single-family homes or condominiums—the more expensive it is to develop. Large tracts were the prize. Large tracts create economies of scale. Developers can spread the cost if they have enough acreage. It helps the development turn a profit.

If I could help KB Home acquire some of Farbod Sattari's holdings, I would come out a winner. I could help Farbod Sattari, and I could help KB Home.

Sitting in Einstein Bros. Bagels with Farbod Sattari and Elizabeth Parker, I had high hopes.

KB Home offered $150,000 an acre. That was the number that Farbod Sattari said would get the deal done.

But Farbod changed his mind.

Like many landowners, he was collecting offers. He wasn't really looking to sell. He knew the 20-acre parcel was a prize.

It turned out that Elizabeth Parker knew Farbod and his reputation. I was surprised that he backed away from the deal. She, however, was not surprised. For some reason I had never encountered the name Farbod Sattari, but his track record for never closing deals was well known all over the Valley.

But, over bagels and coffee, he claimed a neighbor by the name of Jim Zeiter would pay more than KB Home was offering to pay. Jim Zeiter would ultimately become one of the brokers on Bob Combs' pig farm.

My first meeting with Farbod Sattari and Elizabeth Parker proved fruitless. At least, it yielded no sale to KB Home.

From my point of view, the decision to sell or not was Farbod's call. *His choice.*

I knew Farbod Sattari didn't have a broker representing his land. That was baffling. How did someone with so much property in his portfolio not have a broker?

I needed to find an angle into his world. I started dwelling on how I could win such a prize.

I called him four or five times a day. I was persistent. That's who I was. Perhaps by now, you have sensed a trend—whether it was pursuing the job at Southwest Airlines or with New Century Mortgage, I like a challenge.

Many times, Farbod Sattari wouldn't pick up the phone. He knew who it was.

I knew he didn't like being hounded, but I called anyway. There were times when he was super nice. I could tell I was reeling him in. I called him—and called him—for months. I started calling him from new telephone numbers so he would pick up the phone, in case he was intentionally dodging me by blocking my number.

Clearly my approach of hounding him to hire me as his exclusive broker wasn't working. I wasn't making progress. I realized that I would need to think of something creative and innovative. I needed to get his attention in a new way.

One night, I was between sleep and wakefulness. Have you ever noticed that ideas come to you when you aren't thinking about the problem itself?

The idea came to me out of the blue. It was such a great strategy that I was immediately wide awake. I was tempted to call him on the spot, but it was already 11:00 p.m. I forced myself to wait until morning.

The idea was simple: I would start appealing the taxes on all the vacant land he held. He was paying millions of dollars in taxes on all his parcels of land. Anything I could do to get his taxes lowered would be a huge gift. I would do the work for free if I could be his broker when he was ready to start selling.

"Mike—you would do that for me?"

He was immediately intrigued.

"Yes," I said. "I would. Of course."

Soon, he let me into his inner circle. He started telling everyone, "I've got an exclusive broker now. It's Michael Longi."

When I heard this, it was a twofold feeling. I felt satisfied I had landed Omega Family Limited Partnership as an exclusive client. However, the way he bragged to everyone about it was not going to help. He was creating resentment towards me in the brokerage community.

One of those who hated the relationship was a guy named Kay Roohani.

Kay Roohani owned as much land as Farbod Sattari. I did a deal with Kay in 2007 where I represented the Price family on 10 acres of land that they owned in section one of Kyle Canyon Road. Kay was the buyer and in escrow with them and then asked for a price reduction when Clayton Price was on his death bed dying of old age. I knew Kay well. I beat him out of dozens of deals over the years. He beat me out of many deals. We definitely had a history. I liked Kay at the end of the day. He changed how the land game was played in the valley when he came to town. Kay Roohani and Farbod Sattari had been "frenemies" over many decades. Both were hardworking individuals from Iran. Both were taking advantage of all the opportunities this country had to offer people who migrated here from other countries. Now fast-forward over those four decades—between the two of them, they owned a good portion of the Valley.

After I floated my proposal, I became very close with Farbod, his wife Nahid, his daughter Jessamine, and his son Mordred. Farbod told me that I would not be his exclusive broker unless I met his entire family and—this was key—his wife approved of me.

Good news. Nahid liked me.

When I first met Farbod, he joked about me marrying his 18-year-old daughter. I informed him that people don't arrange marriages in this country. That is how much he liked me. Not only did I end up becoming Farbod's broker, but Nahid, Mordred, and Jessamine would all later move their licenses to my company.

. . . .

Farbod also had a suggestion to further complicate our bargaining. I wasn't going to get away with *only* appealing his taxes. He had another favor in mind, a big one that would entangle my life with the Sattari clan in a major way for years to come.

"Hey, Mike," he said. "Would you hire my son? Teach him the land game?"

At the time, of course, I could see all sorts of issues. It's never easy to do a job and show somebody the ropes at the same time. The basics of real estate are not all that complicated, but there is a ton of detail that you need to learn. That's why I went to school to receive the prestigious CCIM designation.

The idea of bringing Mordred in under my wing seemed daunting.

During that first year of contact with Farbod Sattari, he also bought my office building from me. Farbod had asked me to find him an office building and mine fit the bill of what he was looking for. He liked it.

It was a short sale. He bought it for $250,000, but I owed $700,000. I never wanted to short-sale it, but it was on a balloon loan with Bank of America. They wanted their money. I didn't have much choice. I negotiated a short payoff with the bank and had to pay them a substantial amount of money so they would not sue me.

Farbod Sattari's eyes lit up, and I knew he liked the office building for the meager amount of money the bank was asking—$250,000. The appraisal confirmed the asking price, and that's the amount Farbod paid.

It turned out to be a very good investment for him.

CHAPTER 10

My New "Family"

In January 2013, I found out that my assistant Nancy was bad-mouthing me behind my back. Farbod revealed this fact to me. He said he would ask Nancy what she thought of me, and that she would speak negatively. I also caught Nancy looking for another job on the work computer, so I let her go.

I did the firing—and I hate firing people. It's the one part of owning a business I always despise. Mordred watched Nancy pack her belongings. I was very sad about all of this. I actually gave her a severance check of several thousand dollars.

That's when Mordred became my new assistant.

Farbod wouldn't give up on me teaching Mordred the land business. He started calling me, almost the same way I had pursued him. He would even call me on blocked lines.

At the time, Mordred was taking regular college classes at UNLV. (In fact, he took classes off and on at UNLV for years; he never committed to any job for long.) But Farbod told me that if I taught his son the land business, he would let me sell the twenty acres at Hualapai and Farm and that he would give me the entire 6 percent commission.

This is what I wanted! I said yes to the whole teach-Mordred-the-ropes bargain.

Farbod gave me the property to sell, and he told me the asking price was $7 million.

Within a couple of days, I put the twenty acres in escrow with Woodside Homes. I was thrilled. *Ecstatic* might be a better word.

In addition, I put an adjoining fifteen acres in escrow with Woodside Homes that I was brokering for my client, Dr. Rao Yermmasetti. This was a huge assemblage, and it was an all-or-nothing deal. I would sell the whole thing together.

During that period, I flew to Texas and met my daughter Tina for the first time. I had lunch with her in April 2013. I remember bragging to Tina about the big deal at Hualapai and Farm, in addition to the closing with Woodside Homes and all the money I was going to make.

Saying things out loud like that is always a jinx waiting to happen.

Upon my return to Las Vegas, I found that Woodside Homes wanted a zoning contingency. They had a 30-day deal to purchase, and they asked for more time. But Farbod refused, so Woodside canceled the escrow. My client Rao followed suit, and I lost an escrow on around thirty-five acres.

Around that time, I found out this wasn't Farbod's only failed attempt to sell the twenty acres at Hualapai and Farm. Farbod told me he was previously sued for not performing on a contract and ended up paying $550,000 to a developer named Juliet Companies.

When the deal with Woodside fell through, I was crushed. I thought for sure it was going to close. I had already come up with many ways to spend that $800,000 commission. But I was also determined to keep plugging away. I knew I could find an offer that would satisfy Farbod Sattari. But that wasn't the only problem. Mordred was causing all sorts of friction around the office.

Farbod's son was an odd duck. Soon after I hired him, he would say that people were often coming around the real estate office looking for me. He would claim that these people would physically assault him when he did not or could not tell them where I was.

When pressed on this—because it made no sense to me—Mordred

would get violently mad. When I would mention these strange accusations Mordred was making to Farbod and Nahid, they laughed it off.

How could somebody claim he was assaulted and not call the police? How come he didn't look like he'd been assaulted? Why did he tell the same story over and over through the years, always a new assault on a regular basis and never when anyone was around? Why did he become violently confrontational when I asked him for details? I reflected on how Farbod would always speak praises about me around his son. I could see this was creating jealousy in Mordred.

Farbod also gave me a smaller parcel to sell. It was five acres at S. Eastern Boulevard and Pecos Ridge Parkway in Henderson, about seventeen miles south of Downtown Las Vegas. Within a couple of months, I got him a price of $400,000 an acre—full list price. That was an excellent value at the time.

The total was a little over $2 million. I should have known right then and there, from that very first deal, that he was not going to be the greatest client. Why? Because he was already complaining about how unhappy he was with the transaction, even though he had agreed to the price.

"Before the downturn, I was offered a million dollars an acre for that property," he said.

"Yeah, Farbod, that was *before* the downturn. It's a different time now," I said.

It's always the seller's call to agree to an offer. I believe that to my core. I'm a very client-friendly broker. It's not as if I forced him or coerced him into making the deal. So, complaining seemed bizarre to me. Sure, you can have seller's regret, but he was one of the top land owners in the state. He should be familiar with how this works. He called me, complaining about how little he would be getting. I always made it a matter of principle that if someone was not satisfied when they sold a property, then I would let that client go. But I still had the twenty acres at Hualapai and Farm in my sights.

This time, I brought him a price for the five acres in Henderson that people had not seen since the financial crisis, and he was complaining about it—nonstop.

He was the one that dictated the price. *He* was the one that agreed to the terms. What good does it do to complain after the deal has gone through?

I should have seen trouble coming.

. . . .

I kept busy with my other business as the Las Vegas real estate market started to heat up.

For years, I had been known as "The Longinator." It was a self-given nickname for my narcissistic and cocky attitude. I stole it from the movie, *The Terminator*.

I would say things like, "You can't beat The Longinator." People would ask me how I won the deal, and I'd brag about myself using the moniker.

I thought it was all part of the game. "The Longinator" stuck, and I liked it at the time. I knew early on in real estate that you had to believe in yourself, and having a boastful nickname helped.

About once a year I would close a deal for Farbod Sattari. Each deal required a lot of time and effort on my part. One client was consuming over 90 percent of my time. Nothing came easy. No negotiation was ever smooth and straightforward. My concerns about my entanglements and future with Farbod Sattari started to grow. When I closed a deal with Farbod, I would pay his wife half the commissions. She had a real estate license and hung it at my office.

Regardless of the money, I was starting to realize that the hard work and grief might not be worth it.

. . . .

Even with my growing misgivings, I became a frequent visitor to his house. There was part of me that was very proud of the fact that Farbod

Sattari was telling everybody I was his "forever broker." He also told people he considered me family.

I think those comments got under Mordred's skin. I would hear Farbod tell Mordred, "You are never going to broker my stuff. It's always going to be Mike."

These comments got me worried. I wondered what type of psychological effects they were having on Farbod's own son. Why would he say things like that?

Mordred acted aggressively towards me when he said people were coming to the office and assaulted *him* but were looking for *me*. Was Mordred making these comments because Farbod always told him that I was going to be his "forever broker"?

I tried to ease Mordred's concerns by assuring him that he was going to partner with me and that he would get paid when I sold his father's properties. I did not want Mordred hating me because of his father's taunts. Why would Farbod favor me over his own flesh and blood, anyway? It didn't make sense.

We were all out for a buffet lunch on a Saturday at the Red Rock Casino about a year after I became Farbod's exclusive broker. Almost out of the blue, Jessamine asked: "Mike, how did you land our father as a client? There's been a million brokers that pursued him, and you're the first to actually do it."

Farbod was looking at me. Nahid was looking at me. Mordred and Jessamine were looking at me.

So, I told the story about offering to appeal Farbod's taxes. Farbod's eyes lit up. "Mike, that's exactly when you landed me as a client—you're smarter than I thought you are!"

. . . .

Farbod's relationships were odd, and he kept up his taunts to Mordred.

One reason Farbod's son was unlikely to take over my role was that he struggled to pass his real estate exam. I believe it took him nine or ten times to pass. When Mordred failed, he would have rage-filled outbursts and throw tantrums. I was sure Farbod's lack of confidence in his son didn't help.

Every time Farbod said something negative about him, Mordred stood there with a pained look on his face.

. . . .

Over the months, I could see that Farbod had an extensive and sometimes dark history in Las Vegas.

Farbod would tell me stories about how he owned the Italian restaurant where all the Mafia used to hang out. He told me how Sheriff Ralph Lamb gave him a liquor license before he even became a U.S. citizen, a license that was later investigated by the FBI. (Sheriff Lamb was briefly played on a TV show called *Vegas* on CBS. Dennis Quaid played Lamb. As one obituary put it in 2015, after Lamb died: "The two-fisted sheriff was known for facing down bad men eye-to-eye, including mobsters, biker gangs, and killers-for-hire." Coincidentally, I attended Sheriff Lamb's funeral, and I had brokered the 7.5-acre horse corral for his ex-wife near Lake Mead and Jones. I'm also good friends with his son, Cliff Lamb, who referred me to the deal.)

Farbod Sattari told me he was familiar with the code of silence, and he never ratted people out. He would talk about his friendships with Lefty Rosenthal and other past Las Vegas gangsters. I kept getting the feeling that there was another whole side of the Sattaris' family life and their business I knew nothing about.

As I've mentioned, Farbod Sattari was a huge landowner in Las Vegas Valley. At the time we met, he would brag that his holdings totaled $300 million—not bad for a guy who showed up in Las Vegas in the 1960s, working for minimum wage in restaurants. I had to hand it to him. He was doing what many Americans were too lazy to do. He came to this country without a penny to his name, and he went to work. He applied himself.

I think he respected me and my drive. He saw how hard I had pursued him, and that made him realize that I would not back down, that

I would always find a way to make a deal work. He realized that I was one of only a few brokers who were making a killing at real estate, while everyone else around me cried poor mouth. I had never once let the downturn dictate whether I would be successful. Regardless of what happened, I would be one of the last ones standing.

Farbod admired the fact that I came from being a cargo handler, from *nothing*, and that I had a reputation of honesty.

I was also showing Mordred Sattari the ropes. I was selling property, albeit occasionally, for Farbod. Slowly but surely, I was being included in the Sattari family.

I was—*in.*

But was that what I wanted?

. . . .

I told Farbod and his wife early on that if I assembled anything next to something he owned—and if he wanted to be a part of the assemblage—I would bring his family in on the commissions.

In other words, I would share. Very few people in life show that type of generosity. That is who I am. I wanted to be Farbod Sattari's exclusive broker. Farbod commented to me: "God does not let you get burned on deals because you are so generous with people."

A fateful comment.

. . . .

I also realized something very concerning. When Nancy had been my assistant I was suddenly competing—on every potential deal—with a broker by the name of Jim Zeiter. That was the name of the guy Farbod Sattari claimed would give him a better offer than KB Home, way back after our first Einstein's meeting.

In addition to Zeiter, it seemed that I was also suddenly competing with another broker, a former North Las Vegas mayor by the name of Mike Montandon. Montandon had joined Zeiter's firm in 2012. Zeiter was considered one of the true real estate veterans in Las Vegas, with a career lasting three decades at that point.

Farbod told me that Jim Zeiter and Mike Montandon had formed an alliance to go after my business. Every time a good lead came in, I was suddenly competing with these two people.

What was going on?

There was another person involved, a woman named Elaine Eliot. Like Nancy, Elaine Eliot had worked for Aspen Financial Group, which had gone bankrupt during the financial crash.

Elaine would call me on a regular basis asking about properties I had listed at the beginning of 2013. And guess what? Elaine also went to work for Jim Zeiter.

I had a hunch that Nancy and Elaine created a pipeline of information, feeding Zeiter leads coming into my firm. I didn't have proof. But I felt they were targeting me based on how successful I had become. I had built my career on honesty and generosity.

I told Elaine not to contact me anymore. She didn't have a real estate license, and technically speaking, I couldn't discuss properties with her. She got very heated with me on the phone and made a threat that they would pay me back using the Sattaris.

A strange thing to say.

Everyone knew that I had survived the downturn and done very well at a time when others had not. Not only was I selling bank-owned parcels for most of the banks, but I had also survived the great recession without taking too many hits.

Plus, I became the exclusive broker of Omega Family L.P., owned by Farbod Sattari! I had become one of the most hated people in the land brokerage community based on my success. People were jealous of me. Nobody hates you when you're not making money.

. . . .

I kept on selling property occasionally for Farbod.

But Mordred was always there to drag me down. At first glance, he was one of the most likable people you'd ever meet. But it was his dark side, which came out about 1 percent of the time, that creeped me out.

I never said anything to get Mordred to change his behavior or how he acted. I would just walk away. When I mentioned this odd-duck behavior to his parents, Farbod and Nahid would laugh and shrug it off.

In the summer of 2013, Farbod, Mordred, and I attended a tax sale. One of the pieces that was up for auction was located at South Las Vegas Boulevard and Richmar Avenue. The site was 6.61 acres of vacant land. It was a former clubhouse that was part of an older townhome project. The property was lost to a tax sale because the lender did not plan properly. I tracked this property for Farbod and showed him the potential.

The property was bid up the first day to $1.8 million. But I knew it was just a game being played. I also knew that tax auctions run for two days in case there is a default on the payment that's required by 5:00 p.m. by the successful bidder.

I called Farbod that night and told him that I didn't think the potential buyers would show up with the $1.8 million. Sure enough, the next day at the auction, the would-be buyers had defaulted. The auction started all over again. My prediction was correct.

Farbod bid the price up to $1.6 million. Another Iranian in the audience bid it up to $1.8 million, but he was on his cell phone, which was against the rules.

It was Mordred who first noticed the buyer using his cell phone and screamed out he was on his cell phone. I started chanting, "Throw him out, throw him out."

Many others in attendance joined me. Everyone started chanting.

The bidder was thrown out—as well as his bid. I ended up getting Farbod this particular property and helped him beat out his longtime competitor, Kay Roohani. It was Kay who had been directing the bid remotely via cell phone.

This was another chapter in the long-running battle between Farbod and Kay Roohani, and I had helped Farbod score a major victory. It was as if they were having a contest to see who could accumulate the most money in their lifetimes.

I went to Farbod's house after the tax auction and asked him to pay me 3 percent of the sale price of the property. The property had been my listing before the auction. I had tracked the deal for him and went to the auction to handle the bidding process.

To put it bluntly, I deserved compensation for my work.

Farbod became disgruntled, so I asked him for 1 percent instead.

But nothing was ever easy with Farbod Sattari. He didn't agree to that either. Instead, he told me that if I ever wanted to fire him as a client, he would pay me $48,000, the full 3 percent.

I asked him to shake on it and we did.

I was bummed that he did not want to pay me. I had done many months of work for Farbod on this property and had been paid nothing for it. I had made very little money for all the time it took to close deals for Farbod Sattari.

I was frustrated. Who wouldn't be? You're supposed to get paid when you work. I should have been firmer in my negotiations with Farbod Sattari, but I also trusted him. I put my word above everything. I could not fathom that he wouldn't do the same. I believed he would ultimately pay me the $48,000 he owed me.

How ironic that later, I was supposed to make an amount precisely ten times that on the deal for Hualapai and Farm.

. . . .

The following year, 2014, we had a deal on the table for the 20 acres he owned at Hualapai and Farm. Pulte Homes was the buyer. Farbod Sattari signed a letter of intent, and then, when it came to the contract, he refused to sign. He claimed it was too complicated because the contract was over four pages long. He had come to my office, and I shed a few tears in front of him. Farbod Sattari was too much to handle. He was destroying my reputation. He was immediately remorseful, but his remorse didn't last.

I realized right then that Farbod Sattari was a liability. He was having me meet with the City of Las Vegas and wasting an inordinate amount of time on meetings that didn't amount to anything. Farbod would have me go to the city to start working on a zone change for a residential sub-division. This involved lots of paperwork, lots of bureaucracy, and used up lots of my precious time.

The bottom line was we had a deal, and he was not honoring it. Plus, I was honoring my other commitment to him by helping his son learn the land business.

If you accept an offer, why wouldn't you follow through and take the money?

I was baffled.

In the beginning when I was dealing with Mordred's drama, I figured for that kind of potential money, I could put up with the hassle of showing Mordred the real estate business. When I finally understood what type of reputation Farbod had around the Valley, I realized it was impacting the way people saw me as well.

Part of the problem was Mordred's character, but his father could be overbearing too. Farbod didn't make up his mind about land deals like a typical landowner. I thought I had learned to accept that quirk, but now I was growing frustrated.

I figured every landowner has a right to decide when to sell or not. As I have said, that is one of my core beliefs. I don't believe in strong-arm tactics. What I believe is selling parcels of land when the owner is ready to sell. That's all. It's simple. Why would you want unhappy clients or a client who has regrets about a deal? But Farbod Sattari was testing this concept to its limits.

On my end of the bargain—to train Mordred in the real estate busi-ness—the terms were vague. There was no set goal. What did "success" look like? Would it be when Mordred obtained his real estate license? Or when he negotiated a few deals of his own? First, he had to pass his real estate exam, which he had a hard time doing. I don't think I'd ever seen someone take the real estate test more times than Mordred. He had a lazy demeanor, being his father's son and still living at home in his early twenties. He acted entitled about everything.

I had taken Mordred under my wing out of my own good graces to stay close to the Hualapai and Farm opportunity and to show how generous I could be. I even offered to let Nahid Sattari come in on deals of mine if they were properties contiguous to any of Farbod's holdings, as long as he decided to sell those parcels.

In spite of everything, I still wanted to keep Farbod Sattari as a client for life. My offer wasn't entirely altruistic. I wanted the Hualapai and Farm deal to go through eventually.

In fact, I wanted every Farbod Sattari deal. But believe me, I was increasingly wary. Farbod seemed to get everything he wanted. Everything was always on his terms.

God would not let me get burned on transactions because of how generous I was with others. Remember Farbod telling me that?

These words stuck with me. And later they would prove true when it was discovered the Hualapai and Farm listing was stolen.

On one hand, the Sattari family treated me like I belonged. For a guy who dreamed of having his own family someday, it felt fantastic.

On the other hand, I was struggling to figure this family out—especially Farbod and Mordred.

. . . .

These are the two principal characters to keep your eye on: Farbod Sattari and Bob Combs.

Farbod Sattari and Bob Combs represented two major sources of potential for my business.

For me.

And with Farbod Sattari, I thought the opportunity came with a bonus feature that meant quite a bit to me: a family.

At first, I was right. And then I was very, very wrong.

Before we get too much further, however, I need to bring a couple more characters on stage. And when I say "characters," as you'll see, I really mean it.

Their names are Mike Levin and Shawn Lampman.

CHAPTER 11

The "Levinator"

M ike Levin was an unusual man with an unusual history. Notorious?

I think the word fits.

He was a former FBI agent. And a former prison inmate and federal felon.

Levin began work for the FBI in 1989. Five years later, he was suspended for abusing a government credit card. Two years after that, he was suspended again. Same problem.

Similar allegations arose in 1997, and the FBI recommended that Levin be fired. But he resigned instead and went to work as a private investigator; he soon developed a reputation around town for bragging about how much money he was making.

Levin's "good looks and gift for gab made him one of the FBI's better undercover agents," said an article in the *Las Vegas Sun*. "But he also had a penchant for fancy cars and living in the fast lane, as was the case with some of the targets he pursued."

As a private investigator, Levin worked for clients with connections to the criminal underworld—quite a switch from working for the FBI.

On June 13, 2001, Levin flew from Las Vegas to New York City with FBI documents he obtained from a local FBI security analyst. How did those documents come into his possession? He paid for them.

What Levin didn't know was that he was being watched. Levin sold the information for $2,500 plus tickets to a Yankees game. He was promptly arrested.

Levin saw a way to cut his losses. He cooperated with the FBI agents in New York, which led to the arrest of nine more people, including three in Nevada who had allegedly provided him with the classified FBI records. The three charged in Nevada were an FBI security analyst, an investigator in the Nevada attorney general's office, and a municipal court intake service officer. They all sold information to Levin, who, in turn, sold the documents (at a profit) to "criminal targets," the *Las Vegas Sun* explained.

Levin pleaded guilty to conspiracy and obstruction of justice charges. At the time, he told FBI agents that the scheme padded his private detective income by an extra $100,000 from 1999 through 2001. It was no wonder Levin was spotted riding around in a new Porsche.

Among his buyers were those involved in organized crime.

Levin was ultimately sentenced to thirty months in federal prison. In the end, he did twenty-six months behind bars, including twelve months spent in solitary confinement because of his status as a former law enforcement officer.

Once out of prison, Levin went on to own a successful business called The Parking Team that specialized in parking solutions for apartments and HOAs throughout Southern Nevada.

Levin was also co-founder of a popular, and quite controversial, radio show called "Keeping it Real—with Mike and Jeff." One of the regular features on the show was interviews by Levin with ex-convicts. He wanted to bring awareness to the struggles of ex-cons.

Mike Levin also got his real estate license.

In short, between his work as an investigator helping organized crime, his time in prison, and his radio show, he had connections with criminals of all kinds.

He also started a nonprofit called Friends For Felons.org. One of the cases his foundation featured on the radio show was that of former Clark County Commissioner Dario Herrera, who had been sentenced to fifty months in federal prison for his role in accepting bribes in exchange for favorable county zoning and construction projects.

. . . .

I met Mike Levin in 2014 at Farbod Sattari's house. I didn't know who he was until *after* I had kicked him out of our host's house.

Here's what happened.

Mike Levin was pitching a property owned by a prominent broker, Scott Gragson. Gragson was the former mayor's grandson. He was well-connected and from an extremely wealthy family. Mike Levin wanted Farbod to purchase the property and give him 10 percent ownership, *plus* he wanted to make a commission on the sale.

Farbod Sattari called me up, and I could tell he was nervous.

"Come over here," he told me. "I need your help, and I want you to meet someone."

I went over to Farbod Sattari's house. I met Mike Levin, whose name meant nothing to me. What I did know was that Mike Levin was one of the biggest human beings I had ever seen, with forearms the size of tree trunks. He had a big head, thick neck, baggy jowls, and a receding hairline. He was there with another individual, and I listened to Mike Levin explain how he wanted to structure the transaction.

I didn't like the deal—and I couldn't see why Farbod Sattari would agree to the terms. I didn't think Farbod needed any formal partnership, with Mike Levin or anyone, if they weren't putting up any money themselves.

I told Mike Levin that Farbod did not need any partners, and if he wanted to buy that property, he could make the commission and leave it at that. It was good industrial land with a good price, but the last thing Farbod needed was someone as a partner who didn't have any skin in the game.

With that, Mike Levin, and the partner he showed up with, backed off. They left the house.

Farbod couldn't believe it.

"Do you know who that was you just kicked out of the house?" he said. "Who?" I was clueless.

Farbod told me the story. "Oh my God, you kicked him out of my house! He is a connected person," said Farbod.

I wondered why my friend and client hadn't given me a heads-up. I wasn't afraid of people, but I still thought it was strange that he hadn't told me who I was going to meet.

· · · ·

One final note about Mike Levin that was downright creepy. You recall my self-given nickname, "The Longinator," borrowed from Arnold Schwarzenegger's legendary movie character, *The Terminator*.

Shortly after I kicked Mike Levin out of Farbod Sattari's house, I noticed that Mike Levin started a website. What did he call it?

Levinatorsells.com

His website urged potential clients to "Call the Levinator!"

CHAPTER 12

The Second Federal Felon and the Beginning of Turbulence

The twelve months leading up to my car wreck were turbulent and upsetting, to say the least. The year 2015 was full of chaos and trouble.

Something happened early that year that was off my immediate radar. It involved another character who was lurking in the background. He wasn't somebody I knew. Even though he'd been dealing property for a very long time, I didn't know his name. But I soon would.

Shawn P. Lampman.

On January 5, 2015, Shawn Lampman was sentenced to ten months in federal prison for tax evasion. Forty-nine years old when he was sentenced, Lampman had pleaded guilty the previous April for failing to file a tax return and had been ordered to pay $2.5 million in restitution to the IRS. Lampman was a real winner; in court papers, he had blamed his tax problems on substance abuse and a gambling addiction.

This was not Lampman's first tangle with major legal problems. Lampman had been on the board of the homeowner's association for a development called Desert Carmel, about fifty miles south of downtown Phoenix. Fifty-seven Desert Carmel residents and lot owners sued Lampman and his partner, Denver real estate developer Robert Bealmear, in 2007, claiming they used board memberships to enrich themselves at the expense of the community. They claimed the board members—the majority owners—had conspired to drive down property values to acquire more lots at a discount. They planned to re-subdivide and redevelop Desert Carmel, according to claims in the lawsuit. The plaintiffs said the board neglected maintenance and upkeep of common areas, and they had filled a swimming pool with dirt.

Even worse, the plaintiffs claimed Lampman stole $665,000 from the association. In February 2008, the court appointed a special master to audit the association's financial records. The Desert Carmel board made the books available in May 2008—just after Lampman returned all the money.

As the plaintiffs' attorney noted, "It certainly cannot be described as a coincidence."

Lampman's defense for taking the $665,000 was that he had his own personal account at the same bank as the association and that the nineteen separate withdrawals were accidental. Lampman called it "a bank error."

A judge ultimately declared Lampman and Bealmear "grossly negligent" and took away control of the association. The judge put the homeowner's association in receivership in October of 2007.

But wait, there's more.

Shawn Lampman was a longtime associate of Mike Montandon, the aforementioned former Mayor of North Las Vegas. Montandon served as mayor for twelve years, from 1997 to 2009.

Lampman and Montandon met in 1997, bonding over their interest in motorcycles. They briefly formed a company to buy property, a 10-acre parcel. Montandon defaulted on his promissory note, however, and Lampman ended up owning the entire property. The pair have stayed in close touch ever since.

In the early 2000s, Lampman owned a company called Las Vegas Gaming Investments when Montandon's name—and Lampman's—

showed up in an ethics complaint that went to the Nevada Commission on Ethics.

The complaint involved a complicated application by a company called Station Casinos to build a casino on the Craig Ranch Golf Course. Ultimately, Montandon was cleared, but there were many close to the deal who still believed Montandon was helping Lampman gain an inside edge.

Lampman also tangled repeatedly with legal matters in his role with World Series of Fighting. A simple online search reveals a slew of legal struggles over fight contracts as Lampman tried to bring WSOF, which was attempting to compete with the highly successful UFC, to international status.

Trouble, it seemed, followed Shawn Lampman wherever he went and in whatever he did. Little did I know early in 2015, as Lampman headed off to serve his ten months in federal prison, that it would follow me as well.

· · · ·

In March 2015, I was at my daughter's wedding in Driftwood, Texas, a few miles southwest of Austin. It was the Ides of March—the 15th of the month. How ironic I would feel the chill of death on the day Caesar died.

A fateful day for sure.

I have mentioned this wedding and this trip earlier in the story. I was watching my daughter get married (a daughter I didn't even know I had until four years prior to this celebration). My daughter's adoptive parents were there and so was her biological mother, Teresa. I was thinking about the future, and a chill swept over me.

Something very bad is going to happen.

It felt like I was going to die soon. It was an overwhelming thought. It was so overpowering that I left my daughter's wedding. There was music playing, and it was an exquisite and joyful wedding out in the country. Everyone was drinking and having a good time, but I wasn't drinking because I knew I'd be driving. I wasn't in the mood for the party, and I didn't really understand why, but with the feeling that my life was at stake, I felt a desire to leave. I said goodbye to my daughter, took a few photos with her, gave her a hug, said goodbye to Teresa, and left.

I flew home to Las Vegas the next morning.

By that time, I was encouraging Mordred as hard as I could to attend CCIM School (Certified Commercial Investment Member) so he could learn the ropes. CCIM teaches you the tools to sell commercial real estate, and I wanted Mordred to have a top-notch education in the business.

These classes, four classes in all, were over $1,000 each. I was willing to pay for them. Most brokers don't show their agents that type of generosity. I told Mordred knowledge is power, and these classes give you the knowledge to be a very successful commercial real estate practitioner.

And my generosity was repaid how? With Mordred instigating drama with his dad about attending these classes. He didn't want to go. He didn't want to put in the work. Farbod called me up, hysterical and screaming. Unfortunately, this was typical behavior any time Farbod was upset.

I was tired of all the drama Mordred created. I broke down.

It was all too much—all of Farbod's strange behavior when it came to closing deals and now with Mordred as well.

I finally pulled the trigger and fired Farbod.

And I reminded him he made a promise—that if we ever parted ways, he would pay me the $48,000 on the deal I got him for the land at Las Vegas Boulevard and Richmar.

I told Farbod I was done, and I told him to take Mordred with him. I wanted to get rid of his son who had caused all this drama in my life too.

Farbod went ballistic. He started viciously threatening me like I had never been threatened before.

"I'm going to fucking kill you! You're going to die! You won't know what happened! You will die so quick you won't know what happened."

I wanted to calm him down, so I apologized to him for firing him as a client, and I told him I would take him back. I told him I would keep working with Mordred too. I told him to not worry, that we needed to talk this out. He must have threatened my life dozens of times. I was scared. I don't recall all the minute details, but it was a nonstop onslaught at the top of his voice that seemed to go on for hours. Occasionally, one of us would hang up abruptly. Nahid called me and chewed me out as well. I sensed at the time that this fight with Farbod Sattari had something to do with the premonition I had of my death at my daughter's wedding, but I also knew it wasn't the whole deal, either.

"Farbod, I am sorry, don't be upset. Let's not be crazy." I said words to that effect over and over.

Inside, I was thinking, *holy shit, this guy is freaking out.* Everyone was mad at me but not Mordred. It was like they took turns going crazy attacking me.

The next day at work, Mordred came into my office and told me that his father had been in the emergency room all night and that he might have had a heart attack. I was concerned and worried. This went on—daily—for two or three months. I heard constantly about Farbod's poor health and how he was suffering, all because I had fired him as a client for a full five minutes.

"He's not talking to anybody," Mordred would say. "Nobody has seen my dad in a month; he doesn't go out anymore."

That was unusual. Farbod Sattari had properties all over Las Vegas, and he was known for taking everybody's calls. For him to hole up wasn't like him.

Mordred was doom-and-glooming me, telling me how awful things were for his father and trying to make me feel guilty.

A couple of months after Farbod threatened me, I was talking to Mordred on the phone; out of the blue he handed the phone to Farbod, and we patched things up.

I know I have a generous streak in me—and a forgiving streak too.

This time, it was a big mistake.

. . . .

In the summer of 2015, not too long after feeling the chill of death at my daughter's wedding in Texas, the Bob Combs situation changed in a dramatic way.

At first, I thought the situation represented an enormous opportunity. But it led to a huge and messy entanglement.

The situation was deceptively simple. Bob Combs needed a loan, but every bank wanted his entire 180 acres as collateral. The banks were only willing to give him up to a year for repayment. He didn't want to turn over that much property as collateral for a one-year loan, and besides, they weren't going to lend him as much money as he required.

I saw an opportunity to shine brighter than any other land broker on this planet and to win him over. At the same time, I sensed there might be a problem. I had a feeling of dread that this would drag me into something that would be a big problem.

It was a fateful decision. Had I not stepped in and helped him out, I never would have been murdered. Unfortunately for me, I still had my eyes on the prize—the commission from selling the pig farm.

I personally made him the loan.

I offered to lend him $300,000, and we agreed to a three-year term. He then nagged me to increase the loan amount to $500,000. That seemed a bit too high for what he needed, but Combs begged and pleaded.

I asked for twenty acres of this assemblage as collateral. But it was hardly an easy twenty acres to work with. It abutted the pig farm, so it could still mean it was covered in pig feces. It was twenty acres, yes, but it would only be truly valuable when the pig farm sold and started getting developed.

Once I made the loan, I knew I had made a horrible mistake.

I was at Combs' home for breakfast a few days later. The phone was ringing off the hook.

Why so early in the morning?

Something didn't seem quite right. It was around 7:00 a.m.

Bob's wife Janet was there. "That's Mike Montandon interfering with what you have going on with Bob," she said in front of her husband.

What?

My heart sank.

Suddenly, Bob Combs asked me if I would convert my loan to a livestock loan, meaning that the pigs would be the collateral, not the twenty acres of land he put up to back the loan.

I told him quickly, "No way."

Bob Combs was extremely nervous about the twenty acres he'd put up for collateral, and it seemed like he was doing anything in his power to unencumber it.

Why was a former North Las Vegas mayor interfering with my deal? And why would Bob want me to convert to a livestock loan?

After breakfast, Bob walked me to my car and asked me something that still haunts me to this day.

"Do you enjoy hunting?" he asked. "Would you like to go hunting with me some time?"

"I don't hunt," I said.

Once again, I got that overwhelming feeling, that chill, that my life was at stake.

Why would he want to take me out hunting? Alone?

CHAPTER 13

Chaos and Trouble

In addition to giving me the twenty acres of land as collateral on my loan to him, Bob Combs told me I could put that parcel on the market, that I could list it. What was strange was that he only gave me the listing for around three months.

I had a couple of interested home builders who came out and looked at the parcel, but every time I met with Bob Combs to talk about a potential deal, he would ask me to convert my loan to a livestock loan.

I refused. Every time.

His relentlessness reminded me of myself when I was chasing a land deal. Nonetheless, I kept refusing.

I could not believe he turned all our meetings into a discussion about the same livestock loan idea. Over and over. If I ever needed to cash out on my collateral, how was I supposed to foreclose on thousands of pigs?

Suddenly, I felt very worried about the money I had loaned Bob Combs.

Several months later, on January 31, 2016—less than two weeks before my death in the Albertsons shopping center parking lot—Bob Combs called me up with some exciting news.

Suddenly, Combs told me that he had decided to sell the entire farm. *What?* And he wanted me to be his broker for what I did for him.

"No one on earth would have done what you have done for me," he said.

Again, however, he asked me to convert the loan. He was a broken record!

I refused. And then he said he would not honor our agreement for me to sell the pig farm or any deal I brought him unless I agreed to convert my loan.

I was stunned. I had done him a favor—loaning him the money he needed. This was how he was repaying me?

But let's rewind a few months to the fall of 2015. As opposed to Bob Combs, Farbod Sattari was excited about my loan on the pig farm. Farbod, in fact, was very interested in this deal because he saw it as a way to get in on the action.

Farbod Sattari made a living making hard money loans to people. He even bragged he was the "go-to" guy when the Mafia needed a loan during the old days of early Las Vegas, when the Mafia ran the town.

Around the time I made the loan to Combs, I still had the assemblage of properties that I'd put together back in 2013 at Hualapai and Farm. When I first listed it, my clients were asking too much. Probably way too much. By 2015, the values had changed, and the market prices were catching up with what they were asking. In other words, their asking price was no longer unreasonable.

It was exciting. Remember, this was a fantastic collection I had put together. I had fifteen acres in escrow with a client named Rao. I also had the five-acre charter school property with D.R. Horton Homes, and I had a signed letter of intent with Farbod Sattari to go into escrow with D.R. Horton sometime during the first quarter of 2016 on his twenty acres.

My dream of being the top land broker in the entire Valley was becoming a reality. I was going to be the broker on the Combs portfolio, and I was already the broker for the Omega Family portfolio. At that precise moment, it would not have been a stretch to call me the number one land broker in the Las Vegas Valley.

Things were going well.

Or so I thought.

. . . .

The day of closing on Rao's property and the charter school property in October 2015, Farbod's wife, Nahid, approached me. She asked if she and Mordred could get paid on the fifteen acres I was brokering for Rao and for the five acres I was brokering for the charter school next to Farbod's acreage that just closed escrow. Nahid said that Farbod would repay me from the proceeds of the sale of the twenty acres that Omega owned. I was also promised to be the broker on that deal for teaching Mordred the land business. Mordred, for the very first time, was done with college and was going to start acting as a full-time agent. He had finally passed his real estate exam!

This closing was going to generate a commission of around $200,000. Nahid said Farbod would pay me back very shortly on the twenty acres next door that he was going to sell.

When Farbod makes a promise, Nahid claimed, "he never breaks it."

So, I paid Mordred $22,052 on a deal he did not earn. Mordred might have attended one evening zoning hearing about this property, but we hardly needed anyone there when a national home builder has its own attorneys and consultants on hand. Mordred's true involvement had been nothing. I paid him anyway.

And I paid Farbod's wife Nahid $26,552 on a deal she also did not earn.

These checks were written on October 8, 2015. About six weeks later, I knew I had made a mistake.

I was over at Farbod and Nahid's house for Thanksgiving dinner—November 26, 2015.

"Make sure you eat as much as you want," said Farbod. "After all, you are the one who paid for the dinner."

He said it in kind of a mocking way.

Funny—but not funny.

"No," I said. "You're going to pay me back when the Hualapai and Farm deal goes through—you said you always keep your word."

But I knew what he was saying. He wanted to make sure I knew that I would never see the money. There was still lingering resentment from the time I had "fired" him, even if that was only a five-minute parting.

I could feel it. Our relationship was strained.

Farbod had such a big ego; that wasn't something he was going to forget. We had patched things up on the surface, but Farbod Sattari had a long memory.

Farbod now owed me on Hualapai and Farm—especially since I paid his wife and son on a deal next to that one. And it was a deal they did nothing to earn.

He knew it. I knew it.

Farbod signed a letter of intent with D.R. Horton, right before the murder attempt on my life, to sell them the 20 acres at Hualapai and Farm. Also, Mordred had just graduated from college—finally! For the first time in his life, Mordred was now working as a full-time broker. Soon, right before the wreck happened, Farbod was going to owe me nearly $500,000 as my fee for brokering the property at Hualapai and Farm.

I had put in so much work on that deal. I had been patient, and my three years of dedication were finally about to pay off. But there were still issues everywhere I turned. There was noise and conversation that made me feel unsettled, unsure.

Shortly after Farbod became my landlord, he hounded me that my company was not paying enough rent for office space. *Nothing* was ever easy or straightforward with Farbod Sattari. Even after a contract was signed, he would complain about the rent he was receiving.

I told him that he signed me up on a partial lease, which allowed him to have access to the building. If he wanted to give me a lease on the entire building, I told him, I would sign it and pay more money. He always refused this deal. It seemed like he always wanted access to the building even though it was just an investment for him. I never knew why he wanted access to a building he was not using, especially if he could make more money in rent.

This pressure over the rent went on for some time. Every time he brought up the issue, it added to my feelings of being unsettled and unsure.

There was one bright spot among the Sattari foursome, however.

At Christmas 2015, as a gift, I bought Jessamine Sattari ten private lessons from Marcello Nunes, one of my mixed martial arts coaches. Jessamine got heavily into mixed martial arts. She trained all the time. When I had my jaw popped back into place, I found out she was banned from Drysdale Jiu-Jitsu because they wanted Jessamine to roll with people a lot bigger than her. She refused and put her foot down. That is one of the things I loved about Jessamine. She was super stubborn. You could not tell her what to do. She also had a belief in herself that Mordred and Nahid did not share with her. She reminded me more of her father than her mother or brother. She was driven, and she accomplished her goals.

Because Jessamine was a friend and family, I worked with my coach Robert Drysdale and convinced him to let her back in to train. Drysdale said they needed to take a reset with her. It worked. Jessamine became even more of a friend. She felt like a family member whom I loved and cared about. Where Mordred had his moments of quirky episodes and weirdness that I struggled to tolerate, Jessamine and I had a good relationship. She always wanted to sit next to me when I came over to the Sattaris' for lunch or dinner.

She also made a living reading fortunes online. She was a highly-rated psychic. Jessamine was able to do what her own brother and mother could not do. She was able to take care of herself without relying on her father.

When Jessamine was training with my professional fighter friend, I could tell Mordred did not like it. He was becoming jealous. I didn't care. Why should I? Mordred did not rule my life, and I couldn't care less what he thought.

A few days before my car wreck, I brought Farbod to the new house I planned to buy. His eyes lit up. He immediately wanted the house because of the 270-degree view of the Valley from my master balcony.

I could not help myself; I made a comment: "I could piss off my balcony and hit your roof."

On the spot, he offered me a million dollars for my house, but I refused. This was the beginning of February 2016.

I could only take so much of Mordred. When he started working for me, I would spend half a day at my office and work from my house the other half of the day to minimize our time together.

Of course, I also enjoyed working from my house because of my rescue Labrador dogs, who were always happy to have me around.

It was a few days before my murder that Farbod Sattari signed a letter of intent with D.R. Horton to sell his 20 acres at Hualapai and Farm. I was finally going to get paid back for all my generosity and hard work. It was a huge relief.

A couple days before I was murdered, in a fit of anger, Mordred claimed he wanted my lifestyle. He called me when I got home from work. I was buying my new house, and he was jealous. I was about to broker the pig farm and his dad's acres at Hualapai and Farm. He verbally assaulted me for all my success. "I want your lifestyle!"

"That is something you have to work for," I told him. "Not even Daddy is going to hand that to you."

Mordred went into a murderous frenzy. He verbally assaulted me, and I became fearful for my life.

I could not believe it. I had taught him the land business, paid him incredible money he hadn't earned, and now he was screaming at me because I was buying a new house and was successful.

The bottom line? I had never met a more spoiled brat than Mordred Sattari.

When I did nice things for him, he seemed to be one of the most ungrateful human beings I had ever met. Mordred was swearing at me and threatening me. It reminded me of when his father was screaming at me.

"You have to work for my lifestyle," I told him. "You should not have it handed to you. Your dad came from nothing, and now he is easily one of the richest people in town."

I could not believe I just paid this guy $22,052 and now he was threatening me. I was about to make $480,000 on his dad's acreage and broker the pig farm. I could tell Mordred was green with envy.

Of course, I did not know I would be dead in a couple days.

And I certainly did not know I would travel to the afterlife.

And return.

CHAPTER 14

The God Force

The car wreck was no accident.

There were too many coincidences. Far too many.

There's also a possible video confession after the wreck that takes place in the most unlikely of places—the Oasis RV Park—that proves the voice of God.

We'll get to that soon. After I died and came back, I realized all my near-death experiences before the murder attempt were close encounters with death. I realized after I died and came back that a near-death is when the soul is separated from the body.

But first, I want to revisit the moment of my death—a moment that is indescribable in many ways, but I'm going to try again—and then tell you what happened to me with my physical self and my concussion. Then, I'll walk you through all the evidence and the coincidences that show who I believe was behind my car wreck.

. . . .

I was in a universe of pure conscious thought, and I felt God all around me. I realized in a flash that it is this God Force that creates the physical universe we are in. What I call the God Force is what other people refer to as the Holy Spirit. The feeling of being eternally at peace was profound. I felt my cognition burn in the afterlife like a lighthouse in a dark storm. I saw colors in this new universe that didn't exist on our spectrum in the physical universe. It was like being in a fireworks display multiplied exponentially, without the noise. I was viewing all of creation, past, present, and future all at once. Time was an illusion; it was a feedback loop from the past, present, and future, all intertwined. I'm not sure words from our physical universe can do this justice. I felt like I was in the afterlife for two minutes at least. If my injuries shaved twenty or thirty years off my lifespan, these moments were all worth it.

When I crossed over, I saw balls of light. I now know that those balls of light were angelic beings who ascended to the hand of God.

I was serene. I no longer felt any aches or pains from having a physical body.

I became more and more aware of the nature of life and death. I realized I was an immortal spiritual being. It was not just Jesus who is a son of God. I was also the son of God. So are some of the humans that walk this earth. We all come from the same primordial source of creation, but there is too much evil out there to say "all of the humans" are the sons and daughters of God.

I realized *our* existence is how God experiences the universe he created. We are all part of *his* universe. I later came to know that dark matter is consciousness creating the matrix we are in. Knowledge came to me that the physical universe is both simplistic and miraculous.

Life is created so we immortal spiritual beings can live a mortal existence and know what it is like to experience death. Reincarnation exists.

Death is not the end. Death is only the beginning of a never-dying existence of conscious thought. We suffer an eternity of death and rebirth.

Why does the universe expand exponentially quicker and quicker—what force causes that to happen? It's been a longstanding question among astrophysicists. The answer is *consciousness*. It's consciousness that expands the universe faster and faster every year; that's why it's moving faster than the speed of light. It's the God Force that creates the physical universe, occupied by Elohim.

I was aware of the tapestry of time, the fabric of everything around me. I was in a different dimension.

It was an amazing realization. I also felt the power of my immortal soul and felt it hardwired into reality itself. When I was no longer of my body, I looked off into eternity and saw the tapestry of life in all its glory—past, present, and future.

During the brief time I was dead, I was thinking that I could see why people don't want to come back when they cross over. I was waiting for my cognition to dissipate. Instead, the opposite was happening. I was becoming even more aware. My cognition grew in tremendous power.

This wreck—and all that was happening to me—was a profound life-changing experience.

When I was no longer of the body, I was initially horrified. I could not find my body anywhere. Then, I came to the realization that I was dead. Something strange happened. My consciousness wasn't dissipating. It was expanding. I was scared and panicked.

I was looking for my body, but I couldn't find it. I was not *of* my body. *Where's my body? Where's my body? Why can't I find my body?*

After a moment, a clear thought came to me.

Wait. If you don't have a body, you must be dead.

I felt so peaceful, the last thing I really wanted to do was come back. It felt natural existing as an immortal spiritual being.

In some ways, these ideas and observations may sound narcissistic. I felt that the universe was here for me which is why I made the comment that the universe is here for me. That's a very narcissistic thought.

The balls of light—those ascended beings—may be angels that subside on a higher plane of existence than others. They could clearly see events unfolding in life, yet humanity was unaware of their presence. Those whose sacred name are the Elohim.

When I decided to come back, I thought, *how could I be dead in a shopping center parking lot?* I was thinking of the pig farm, Hualapai and Farm, and also the new house I was purchasing. I thought of my rescue dogs at home and my grandmother who was all alone. Eternally at peace or not, I was not ready to leave my life behind. That was when I started whining about not wanting to die.

And that was when I felt my soul come back through my body, like a sucking sensation through the crown of my head.

It was powerful.

That is how I know it was not some delirious dream. I felt the return of my consciousness and felt my consciousness take control of my limbs. I did not feel the same. Something seriously changed inside me. It was as if my brain was entirely rewired.

Suddenly, I was back inside my car with my foot on the brake at that four-way stop sign. I felt a profound anxiety. All the apprehension I had felt about my upcoming audit and the IRS had been multiplied exponentially. I was shaken up. In fact, I was in shock.

I heard a crackling voice from heaven.

This was no accident. This was meant to kill you. It has something to do with the Sattari family.

That was followed by a chorus of laughing voices fading off to the heavens. I did not believe the chorus or anything that had just happened. In fact, I fought with the voice.

"This is bullshit!" I said. "None of this shit just happened! I love everybody in the Sattari family. I know it couldn't be them! I want proof," I heard myself say to that voice of God when he revealed what happened to me after my soul returned to my physical body.

When I felt sins pulled from me and the chill of death, I realized I needed to listen to that voice.

When I got out of my car, I was grabbing my neck. The driver of the vehicle that hit me was outside already. The first thing he said: "This was an accident, I didn't even see you." What an odd thing to say. There were no skid marks, as he made no attempt to stop when he plowed into me.

Next, he insisted on calling an ambulance, and I could tell he was trying to control the situation.

I refused. I did not have time to get brutally injured! I did not have time to die! I just wanted to move on in life.

When we pulled in front of the Del Taco to exchange information, the driver of the pickup wanted me to lie about what happened by saying I was moving when I reported to my insurance company.

I was utterly horrified. I defiantly told him that was not what happened, as I was fully braked. He started screaming at me, trying to intimidate me. I sensed something strange about the driver, as if he knew exactly what it would take to create a deadly car wreck. I felt fear for my life, and I got the hell out of there. The same chill coursed through my body as when the universe had judged me.

I remembered all of Mordred's violent encounters with me, and his threatening of my life a couple days before, and the times Mordred claimed someone was assaulting him, trying to get to me. I thought of the time Farbod threatened to kill me when I fired him as a client, and then quickly put it out of my mind.

Yes, it was true that I had many concerns about the Sattari family. But in the moment of the car wreck, all I had were thoughts of love for them. I set out to prove the voice of God wrong, but I also knew that if the voice of God was right, then I would have to find the link between the Sattari family and the driver of the pickup.

Also, with my new vulnerability and new sensitivity to the universe, I knew one thing for sure, deep down: that something fundamental had changed about my character. My very being. My sense of myself and my place in the universe.

It was this:

The Longinator had been terminated.

CHAPTER 15

Real Estate Deals Lost

After the wreck, I was a new man. It felt as if I had entered the Twilight Zone. I knew I could not tell anyone about my near-death experience. I had to investigate things for myself before I revealed what truly happened. Being murdered and coming back to this life made me feel victimized on a scale unimaginable. I felt violated. and the last thing I wanted was for whoever was behind this to have the satisfaction that they hurt me. Also, as a safety mechanism, I did not dwell on my near-death experience and did not complain about the motor vehicle collision until a few days after it happened. I wanted to downplay it to find those responsible.

However, it would take me some time, effort, and initiative to figure out precisely what had happened to me and who was involved.

One of the first things that occurred right after my death was Farbod Sattari refusing to go into contract with D.R. Horton after he agreed to sell them his property at Hualapai and Farm. Right before my death, Farbod signed a letter of intent, and he was going into contract. Yet all of a sudden, he canceled the contract after he agreed to sell them the property. Did this have to do with the fact I was still alive? The idea freaked me out, so I tried not to dwell on it. It is why I paid Nahid and Mordred all that money to begin with on the contiguous 20 acres I brokered back in October 2015—I was getting paid back on Farbod's site next door. I reflected on the voice of God, this had something to do with the Sattari family. I would want more proof than Farbod just backing out of a contract.

And on top of these disappointments, there was that newspaper article that announced Mike Montandon would be the broker on the pig farm.

This happened just a few days after my wreck. When that article came out, I had an overwhelming feeling that Mike Montandon had a hand in my murder. So profound was that feeling that it crept down my spine like the icy tentacles of death. The coincidences were startling with Montandon being the new broker on the pig farm. How was Mike Montandon tied to Farbod and Mordred Sattari? The voice of God said it had something to do with the Sattari family. I could not put it together. Farbod did tell me about how Jim Zeiter and Mike Montandon created some unholy alliance to go after my business. Would Mike Montandon resort to murder? I reflected on Bob Combs relentlessly trying to get me to change my collateral on the loan from the 20-acre parcel to a live-stock loan. The idea sent shivers down my spine.

A colleague of Mike Montandon, who worked at Nevada Title, started visiting my office right after my wreck. His name is Travis Nelson. He would give me a buyer lead for my Warm Springs and I-15 listing, and then he would ask how my neck was and start smirking. I felt a deep chill run down my spine when he did this; I felt he knew much more about my wreck than I did. He did this on three occasions, which after the third, he became ghosted by me. I blocked him from communicating with me. When I ghosted him, he became upset that a buyer he referred me went into escrow on some land I had listed. Travis left me a voice message on January 17, 2017. "Mike, Travis Nelson, hey bud, hope you're doing well, hope your neck is feeling better, and I want to touch base with you on the 9 acres on Warm Springs and I-15." The rest of the message talks about him being bummed out that he did not get an escrow with Prologis since he gave me their contact information. Travis and Mike Montandon worked together for many years at Nevada Title. They were connected. What did he know about the driver that tried to kill me? Why the taunting about my neck?

There were two things I needed to understand. One had to do with my medical condition. I spent the first few weeks after the wreck trying to deny that there had been any significant harm done, even though there were clues all around me.

The second had to do with coming to realize that the wreck was no accident.

I need to take you to a business meeting that happened shortly after the collision, in an unusual place. The invitation to this meeting came from a man who had been in the outer circle of my immediate business associates but who was quickly gaining more prominence.

Ray Ghouli was a real estate broker who was associated with dozens of companies. He was also one of the owners of the Oasis RV Park, a sprawling operation a few miles south of McCarran International Airport in Las Vegas, right next to I-15. He was Farbod Sattari's business partner.

Oasis RV Park is no ordinary park. It looks like a fancy resort. There's a family pool with waterfalls. There's an adults-only pool and spa. There's an 18-hole putting course on natural greens. Security runs twenty-four hours a day, and a guard at the front gate checks who belongs and who does not. This "RV park" has a fitness center, horseshoe pits, a laundry, free showers, complimentary Wi-Fi, a restaurant, banquet facilities, and a fully stocked convenience store.

It's huge. There are 935 sites. It's a cash flow machine, and it sits on prime land. Certainly, the value of the land alone is tens of millions of dollars.

Farbod Sattari told me that a wealthy individual out of Beverly Hills gave Ray Ghouli 10 percent ownership in Oasis RV Park, with the idea that Ray would manage it for him.

Until my wreck, I had always thought of Ray in a positive light.

Years earlier, I had met Ghouli at the Clark County Land Auction, which had been held at the County Building. He was kind to me. He had purchased some acreage that was contiguous to a site at Las Vegas Boulevard and Richmar. It was across the street from the property I helped Farbod Sattari purchase at the tax auction. Ray Ghouli had been worried about Kay Roohani purchasing the property, and I had told Ray not to worry about it because, after the financial crisis, cash was king. I was correct and Ray got the property.

In 2014, I had listed some land for my attorney's client and one of the parcels happened to be contiguous, on the north end, to a shopping center owned by Ray Ghouli and his group. He purchased approximately an acre for $300,000. This would be a home run for anyone who purchased the property at that price, but I decided to give this deal to Ghouli, who ended up selling in 2017 for around double what I sold it to him for.

It was one day after the wreck—February 11, 2016—when Ray Ghouli engaged me with a signed letter of intent to purchase some land I had listed, about 9.5 vacant acres, at Warm Springs at I-15.

This was *one day after my wreck.*

The name of the seller I was representing was Rao. Ironically, this was the seller with whom I had sold and closed a deal with on October 7, 2015—and this was the property that led me to pay Nahid and Mordred a share of the commission (which, of course, they did not earn).

Rao countered the LOI immediately, and then we went into contract. Two months later, in early April, Ghouli backed out of the deal.

But before that deal fell apart, Ghouli invited me and my client, D.R. Horton, to the Oasis RV Park to purchase a small parcel of land. It was right after Farbod Sattari backed out of the transaction to sell D.R. Horton his Hualapai and Farm property after he agreed to sell.

I met with Ray and two individuals from D.R. Horton, Matt Stark and Brad Burns. Brad was president of D.R. Horton in Las Vegas. Matt oversaw land acquisitions. We met at Ghouli's private, modest office at the Oasis RV Park.

I reflected on the voice of God: *This has something to do with the Sattari family.*

Farbod and Ray were co-managers of thousands of acres together in West Wendover. Was Ray causing a distraction away from Farbod Sattari backing out of the Hualapai and Farm transaction? My new heightened intuition from PTSD was telling me this was the case. I did not yet know that PTSD was a sort of heightened intuition, but would learn this fact later on. This was days after Ray Ghouli reached out to me with the offer for Warm Springs and I-15.

After some negotiations, which are always par for the course, Ghouli worked out a deal to go into escrow on the sale. D.R. Horton wrote up a letter of intent.

And then, right at the same time the Warm Springs deal fell apart, Ray Ghouli also backed out of the deal with D.R. Horton.

It's likely that Ray Ghouli's greed factor kicked into gear. He was always looking for more money and likely thought he could get a better price by waiting. To me, it seemed like a big distraction from Farbod backing out of Hualapai and Farm.

But the way he backed out of the deal was as startling as when Mordred told me that his dad did not want to sell Hualapai and Farm, which was also after his father informally agreed to go into escrow with D.R. Horton right before my car wreck with a signed letter of intent. I had a signed letter of intent to purchase that was agreed upon by Ray and now he backed out of the deal like Farbod. Both agreed and then backed out.

My meeting at Oasis RV Park was only a day or two after Mordred told me the bad news about Hualapai and Farm. It was as if Ray was putting a false carrot in front of my face. When I had the meeting with Ray at the Oasis, I felt a vulnerability and a great sense of shock, like the wreck just happened a second ago. I was also in a frail state. I was losing a lot of weight. After the meeting, my CPA started telling people I would need to retire medically. It was as if he was getting this from Ray Ghouli—we both share the same CPA. Las Vegas is a really small town.

Farbod would call me every night before my car wreck, and now he was not calling me at all.

What was going on? I felt like I was being jerked around like a yo-yo.

CHAPTER 16

Kimberly

When I started doing kenpo karate in 2010, there was another excellent fighter there by the name of Robert Sigler. He would get his black belt four years later. Sigler was a big-time businessman with a company called Global Trust Group that made its money through mergers and acquisitions.

Sigler's right-hand person was a woman named Kimberly Toy.

Kimberly was a regular at the dojo too. She was very attractive, had a great smile, dark hair, and a dark complexion. I developed a crush on her. I asked her out from time to time, and finally, years later, she agreed. This was in 2015, a few months before the car wreck.

We got involved. We were seeing each other five or six times a week. We started dating more seriously and grew closer.

Kimberly became a big part of my life. She was a truly wonderful and giving person; I loved how she took her brother's kids to karate. She was good to her brother and family. When I say everybody loved her, it's true. She was a joy to be around, and she had a heart of gold. Kimberly would always tell me that if something happened to her, she was going to take care of her family financially.

A couple of days before the car wreck, we were snuggling in my bedroom, watching Netflix. She wanted to watch a true crime documentary series that was very popular at the time, "Making a Murderer." That was not a show I was interested in watching. It had something to do with cops in Wisconsin setting someone up for murder, and it didn't interest me in the least.

That night with Kimberly, I had other things on my mind—more physical things. She referred to it as "playtime." Perhaps I was being too pushy, or it was because I was reluctant to watch the documentary. Whatever the reason, Kimberly got a little huffy.

"Mike," she said, "all I want to do is watch this show and you just want playtime."

She stormed out of the house.

It was our first little squabble. I immediately felt bad about it and how selfishly I had behaved.

But I also wanted to wait a day or two to call her. In fact, I was probably hoping that she would call me. I didn't want to be the one crawling after her. Maybe it was a case of pride—I don't know.

Two mornings later was the car crash. As you can imagine, I was incredibly shaken up by the life altering event. I was so beat-up inside that it felt like I'd taken a Black Belt test. I didn't feel well at all.

I had a deep feeling of anxiety that wouldn't go away.

I told myself that I'd wait a few days to call Kimberly. I wanted to feel better before I called her. I wanted to feel less anxious and more normal, although at the time, I had no idea how long a process that would become.

I was fighting with the voice of thunder and lightning. I told myself that boxers get knocked out all the time, and they don't run to the hospital. I told myself I would feel better soon. I told myself to give it time. However, I had never heard of anyone getting knocked to the afterlife; perhaps my injury was worse.

At the same time, I wanted to move on in life. I was about to broker Combs' pig farm and Hualapai and Farm for Farbod Sattari. My focus, such as it was after the wreck, was on those deals.

Then Mike Montandon was announced as the broker on Combs' pig farm in the *Las Vegas Sun*. I felt a paralyzing fear that he was intertwined with the driver who tried to kill me. But I was confused because the voice of God had told me it had to do with the Sattari family.

I was flabbergasted. I called Bob Combs incessantly. I had had hundreds of conversations with him over the years, but now he would not answer the phone. I called his office, but the phone just rang and rang.

I said to myself, *what a jerk*. The voice of God did say it had something to do with the Sattari family. What a creepy coincidence. My PTSD went off.

"Why do I have that feeling now?" I asked myself. It would be over a year later when I would find out that PTSD is a form of enhanced intuition.

. . . .

I vaguely remember being bedridden for about a month, but one thing I did before deciding to lay low was get my car repaired. Because I had not gone to the doctor immediately after the wreck, and because the driver of the pickup agreed 100 percent to my version of events around the incident, the driver admitted 100 percent liability. As a result, I did not have to pay my deductible for repairs to my car. But the driver's admission of 100 percent liability would play a major role in my future litigation with the owner of the truck, Wadman Corporation, and the driver who sent me to my Maker.

Something was seriously wrong, however. No matter how many days or weeks went by, I had an inescapable feeling, like the wreck just happened a second ago. I was wasting away. Where before my memory was sharp as a tack, it now seemed I was much more forgetful.

It was time to take care of myself and see a doctor, which turned out to be a horrific and nightmarish process all by itself.

I kept waiting to contact Kimberly. I wasn't feeling better like I thought I should, and all sorts of strange things were happening around me. I just lost the pig farm listing and all the land contiguous to it Bob Combs owned for some reason, and what was even stranger was that Bob Combs suddenly stopped asking me to convert the collateral on my loan to a livestock loan. Given how relentless he'd been about it before, this seemed weird. And Farbod Sattari had pulled Hualapai and Farm, even after agreeing to a deal with D.R. Horton. Would he have gone into escrow if I had not returned to this life in that parking lot? I did not want to think about the answer.

I finally called Kimberly, and we agreed to meet at the Marrakech Restaurant off Paradise Road near the Hughes Center. It was a great place, complete with belly dancers. I took an Uber down there because I now had a fear of driving. I developed severe PTSD after I died and had a hard time getting behind the wheel of a car. It was March 25, 2016. Six weeks had passed since I had died.

When she saw me, Kimberly's jaw dropped. My movements had become much more animated than usual. I rambled on without a filter.

I had lost sixty or seventy pounds in a short amount of time. I knew something had happened to me on a very deep level. Kimberly's reaction to my appearance confirmed that the changes had been profound.

When we were dating, Kimberly said she was also seeing an attorney friend. So maybe I knew down deep that I wasn't in the driver's seat in this relationship—and of course I knew that there had been a long gap in time.

Later, when we left the restaurant and belly dancers, Kimberly gave me a ride, and we went to the Red Rock Casino in West Las Vegas. I remember reaching out to hold Kimberly's hand. That was something I had done in the past. She jerked her hand away. Clearly, we weren't going to reconnect at that point. I knew it had been my fault for not calling right away or going after her the night she left my house, when all she wanted to do was watch the documentary on Netflix.

After the awkward meeting at the restaurant and the clear rejection at Red Rock Casino, I tried reaching out to her in the days that followed. But she made it clear that she was in another relationship. She had moved on.

I was crushed. I was all alone now dealing with a serious injury.

Mostly, I was mad at myself. I had lost a chance to be with a truly wonderful woman. Kimberly was one of the only women who didn't seem interested in my financial success at all. In fact, she would give me a hard time if I started to brag about my money. She told me she liked me because of how I fought as a mixed martial artist. She thought I was a "badass." She had dated me for who I was, not how much money was in my bank account. She was just the kind of non-superficial woman I needed. And I'd ruined my shot.

I put the Kimberly Toy chapter behind me, much to my regret. The entire story with her, however, wouldn't close for a few years in a moment that would break my heart.

CHAPTER 17

Eternal Darkness

Let me tell you a story that shows the extent of the injury to my brain. The story captures my transformation, the way it impacted me on a physical basis.

I headed to my attorney's office right after the wreck. I was meeting with Kent Greene and his paralegal, Gloria Setoni. When Gloria looked at me and found out what had happened, she insisted that I immediately go to the ER.

I declined. I felt shaken up, no question about that, but I felt like I could function. Still, I had the distinct feeling that the car wreck had happened a second ago.

I did not know it at the time, but this was a sign of Post-Traumatic Stress Disorder (PTSD). Later, I would learn that people who do not pass out from violent car collisions suffer very severe forms of PTSD. Mine became one of the most severe forms as I experienced life-to-death and death-to-life without losing cognition.

Kent and Gloria argued over a critical issue dealing with the IRS audit. The issue had to do with whether I was allowed to broker assets for a property my pension had loaned money to.

Suddenly, I said something incredibly out of place. "You guys need to argue that on your own fucking time!" (My recollection was this conversation happened right after my wreck. Gloria's recollection is that this happened around a week later.)

My hand immediately covered my mouth. I could not believe I'd just said that.

They both looked at me, startled.

I did not realize it at the time, but that was the first sign of the filter damage I suffered because of the violent shaking of my brain that took place from the murder attempt on my life.

Immediately after the crash on that February day, I returned home and did not feel right. I started becoming reclusive. Bedridden. To this day, I do not remember the first month after the wreck much at all. I was seriously hurt, but other than the fact that I was rapidly losing a massive amount of weight and suffering from what appeared to be an increased sense of anxiety, you couldn't really see the injury.

My head wasn't in the right place. For instance, I would go to pay bills, and every time, I would go from one room to the next; I would forget what I had intended to do. "Pay your bills," I would tell myself. I would get up and walk to the next room, but in that short time, I would forget why I was there. It was an overwhelming feeling of disorientation.

The day after the wreck, I went to work at an obscene time: 4:00 a.m. I wasn't sleeping, so why not go to work? Again, it was that shock sensation. It was bizarre. I remember staring at my computer and feeling out of sorts.

I became sick, but whether from a cold or the injury, I did not know. I was barely able to leave my bed. When I finally dragged myself to the office during normal business hours—I'm not even sure if it was days or weeks—there were three people there: Mordred, Mike Gonzales, and a guy named George Greiner. Greiner was someone I grappled with at Drysdale Jiu-Jitsu. He had moved to Las Vegas from California with his girlfriend, who was an attorney. Three weeks before my car wreck, Greiner asked to hang his license with my real estate company, and I agreed, but he was never one of my employees, only an independent contractor.

Mordred and Mike Gonzales saw me, and they were horrified by my gaunt and wasted appearance.

"Mike, wow," said Mordred, stating the obvious. "You were really hurt."

Farbod and Nahid also saw me and were equally horrified. They begged me to come over, but I was more reclusive than a turtle. For some reason, when I was around Mordred, Nahid, and Farbod, it felt like they knew something I did not. I had the willies around them.

But Farbod and Nahid were reaching out to me. They appeared to be worried about me. They told me that Mordred was accidentally dropped down a couple flights of stairs when he was a kid and suffered a traumatic brain injury—and so had Jessamine when she was in a car collison.

Dropping Mordred down two flights of stairs sounded like a bunch of bullshit. It was if they were trying to strike up some type of rapport over what had happened. They said Mordred had a grapefruit-sized knot after his fall. *Really?* It sounded extreme and made-up.

I noticed there was a change in how I felt about Mordred, Nahid, and Farbod. I now got the creeps every time I was around them. It did not feel right. It was as if they were all keeping a secret from me. I was going nuts thinking about these people who had adopted me into their family. I remembered so clearly that the voice of God told me the wreck had something to do with the Sattari family; I reflected on the coincidences. First, there was Mordred, who often yelled at me uncontrollably and had viciously assaulted me a couple days before the wreck, claiming he wanted my lifestyle. And then there was Farbod, who, when I fired him as a client, said he would kill me so quick I won't know what happened. There was also the driver, who tried to assault me when I did not agree to insurance fraud. And again, there was Mordred, who had been claiming for years that people were assaulting him when looking for me.

I did not have a good vibe around George Greiner or Mike Gonzales either. The one person who did not throw off the creeps was Jessamine Sattari—so I hired her in May 2016.

I wanted to get my money back for what I paid to Nahid and Mordred. It was a substantial amount of money. Most individuals would honor their commitment to pay back a debt.

I was known for keeping my word. It was this part of my character that made me trust the pig farmer, who said I would be the broker of the pig farm when I loaned him a half-million dollars. Bob Combs told me that I would sell the pig farm, so I believed him. That is who I am. I also had nearly a 15-year friendship with Bob Combs when the car wreck happened.

I put the crash out of my head. I did not want to think about what had happened to me. I wanted to get paid what I was owed and try to figure out what scumbag might have been behind this. I knew it was all about finding the connection between the driver and those behind the wreck.

I was very protective of the Sattari family at first. If others had done this to me, what would they do to my adopted family, the Sattaris? I was going into private investigation mode. I did not want the same thing to happen to them.

· · · ·

I never told anyone about the driver asking me to

I disappeared and holed up at my house. I did not mention the wreck to anyone.

I was at home when I finally spoke about what happened to me, talking to Mike Gonzales and Mordred Sattari on speaker phone. I remember Mike making a smug comment about an insurance claim. I heard Mordred giggling. It sent shivers down my spine.

With Mike Gonzales, everything in life was about money. He did not believe in God, only what he could see. When God would come up in a conversation around the office, he was an outspoken critic against him. He never would have been one to show much empathy over somebody getting hurt, especially someone who was more successful than him. I finally told them both that I had been plowed into by a huge construction pickup truck while I was fully braked. I did not mention the assault or the insurance fraud the driver wanted me to commit after I was killed. I played the wreck down. I did not want to come across as someone who was a victim. I did not want the driver and those behind it to know how badly he hurt me.

Some powerful intuition told me to remain silent on the experience of crossing over—of dying and coming back. I was also going to remain silent about my message from my Lord Elohim. That would be my secret and my secret only for the time being. Things would be revealed in time.

But I needed to find the connections to the wreck. I called it "the bridge." I wanted to see how the pieces came together. I took on a new role—that of Inspector Clouseau. But I was not playing a humorous role or trying to make anyone laugh. I really wanted to understand the connections. I was challenging God for proof. I felt that the Sattaris did not know the driver who plowed into me. If only I could find the bridge, everything would eventually be revealed.

But I had heard that voice.

This was not an accident. This was meant to kill you. This has something to do with the Sattari family. Followed by that chorus of laughing voices fading off to the heavens.

It took me several years to come around to realize what was really going on.

It was when I moved into my new house in May 2016 that I contemplated suicide. I was defiant in my prayer to God. I had not seen any sign of Hell when I was dead. If the lower world didn't exist, then why stick around this horrible place?

That night I ended up in a deep sleep. In my dreams, I was being led down a glorious white marble corridor, and into a courtyard. I had the feeling I was in heaven and in the afterlife. I was then shown a guardian suited up in armor with his hands on a long broadsword. The guardian was giant in stature. He wasn't scary, however. It was the portal he was standing next to that made me fearful. It was the opposite of consciousness. It was the void. So absent of light and consciousness. It was an unfathomable darkness. I immediately woke in terror. I'd gazed into the portals of Hell, or what others would refer to as eternal darkness. It was not a place I wanted to occupy. I immediately woke up in a paralyzing fear.

I was no longer going to contemplate suicide as a result of my depression. I was shown a powerful vision and was not going to question it. I was now going to deal with life and all its challenges and not take an easy route out of this world.

CHAPTER 18

Strange Occurrences After My Murder

In July 2016, I got a call from Farbod Sattari offering me a chance to get a big listing. I'll call it West Wendover—a town on the Utah/Nevada border, about a six-hour drive north of Las Vegas. Ray Ghouli and Farbod Sattari had split managerial control of the listing, 50 percent each. Farbod wanted to get rid of all the businesses where he was entangled with other partners.

The asking price was $30 million, so the available commission would be a tidy $1.8 million. Obviously, I was very interested in that commission, but I also thought it was coincidental that Farbod was dangling this deal in front of my face only a few months after canceling the sale on Hualapai and Farm, and the other deal with Ghouli falling through.

Finally, I proposed to Farbod that Ray Ghouli get half the commission. Farbod fought me over that proposal. I told Farbod he would have to play on Ray Ghouli's human greed factor and cut him in on the deal with 50 percent of the commission.

Regarding my 50 percent, I would also have to split my share of the commission with those names on the listing—Nahid Sattari, Mordred Sattari, George Greiner, and Mike Gonzales. I wanted everybody to be involved. I treat others the way I want to be treated. The property wasn't worth $30 million, so it was unlikely that anything would come of it, but the discussion led to the second meeting at the Oasis RV Park.

In October 2016, I went to the Oasis RV Park and sat in Ray Ghouli's modest office one more time. Mordred accompanied me. It had been eight months since I died and came back, and I felt compelled to mention the wreck. I did not mention the driver assaulting me or trying to get me to commit insurance fraud, nor did I reveal my sacred message from God.

"I hope you can still function," Ghouli said. Then, Ray Ghouli looked over at Mordred and winked.

I was horrified. It felt as if he knew something that I did not know.

The wink at Mordred sent me on edge. My PTSD went on high alert. What did Ray know about my death? I then started thinking of how it seemed certain people in the Valley knew of my wreck.

As soon as I saw the wink, I started thinking about how, before the wreck, Ray had treated me with kindness and respect, yet after the wreck, he complained about me more than any other person. Where did this sudden, deep-seated hatred towards me come from? Did it spring from a failed murder attempt on my life?

When I was marketing the West Wendover land for Ray and Farbod, I was the only one Ray complained about—yet I was the only one spending money on the listing. In fact, I was spending substantial money on it. At one point, I was investing more than $3,000 a month. Ray Ghouli should have been appreciative of my efforts, not defaming me. Farbod would tell me every time Ghouli called him to complain about me. This disturbed me deeply. Being around the Sattari family was about as weird and strange as being around the Addams Family, except for Jessamine.

I left this second meeting at the Oasis RV Park with a feeling of great fear and apprehension. I had the listing agreement and started marketing the property. But nothing ever came of it.

Yet another fat carrot dangled in front of my face by Farbod Sattari that went nowhere.

. . . .

But 2016 wasn't done delivering rough news.

In November, nine months after I died, Bob Combs sued me. Out of the blue. Well, maybe not completely out of the blue. We had been tussling. Combs filed the lawsuit on November 16, but I wasn't served and had no knowledge of the lawsuit until January 2017.

Combs went to court because I wanted my share of the commission from the sale of the pig farm. As you recall, shortly after the wreck, I discovered that Combs had signed Mike Montandon to serve as the broker on that property, completely behind my back and in violation of the agreement we reached: that I would be his exclusive broker on the property and his future broker on the entire pig farm. All of this was agreed to when I loaned him the $500,000 in August 2015.

It's true that Combs gave me a brief window (from about September 10 through December 31, 2016) to sell the twenty acres, but I was never able to sell the property because every time I brought him a potential buyer, he would only talk to me about converting my loan. Every time he would say this, my heart sank. I felt like I was being conned. I had buyers interested in land in North Las Vegas, but he would never take any of the offers I brought him. We always met at the Bagel Café or a Denny's, and he had only one thing on his mind—converting the loan. Every time he brought this up, the hairs on the back of my neck would stand up. He never let me come to his house for a meeting after the first breakfast we shared after the loan.

Combs had never told me he would give the listing to another real estate broker, let alone Mike Montandon. It turned out that Combs gave Montandon the listing on February 22—just twelve days after my wreck.

In April, Montandon found a buyer. In July, I submitted my request for the share of the commission that was due to me. Combs denied my commission claim. Later, in the lawsuits, Combs claimed I waited too long to ask for my share. He claimed that I had taken down my "for sale" signs, after my brief three-month listing window expired. He asserted that by taking down the signs, I understood I was no longer the listing agent. Combs also claimed that I was extorting him, that I was looking to delay the closing, and that I was defrauding the title.

In March 2017, I countersued Combs. I hit him hard. I called him out for all the misleading statements and lies in his lawsuit, and I pointed out something I had discovered through my own digging.

In March 2016, I had called the Clark County Recorder's Office to check on the transfer of one of the Combs' parcels to a new living trust. It was the 20-acre piece that was my collateral. All of the Combs' properties were transferred to a new living trust, with the exception of my collateral. My note had what is called a due-on-sale clause, which means I am to be paid off if there is a transfer of ownership. Upon further inspection online, I discovered the piece was transferred to the new trust but then deceptively covered up. I discovered the transfer happening when, out of the blue, Bob Combs emailed me: "I will never forget what you did for me."

I immediately had the willies about my collateral. When I went online, the transfer had just happened minutes before. When I asked them for the trust documents of the new owner, Combs informed me the transfer never happened. The Recorder's Office told me that a quit claim deed had been filed that transferred the title from Combs' name to a living trust called Babe's Silk Purse Trust. However, the Recorder's Office also told me, the recording was later deleted online. Like it was intentionally covered up.

Learning that, I once again asked for all the trust documents from Combs to protect my collateral.

Montandon worked at Nevada Title while he was mayor of North Las Vegas. He knew the title process and the recording process. My intuition told me that Combs conspired with the title company and Montandon to convey ownership from Combs to Babe's Silk Purse Trust in order to impair my collateral for the $500,000 loan. If I had taken a deed in lieu of foreclosure after this recording happened, then my loan would be wiped out, and Combs' trust would become the new owner without the half million I lent him. I saw the deception for what it was. It was as if my PTSD was a super-enhanced "spider sense" reading into the future.

My commission claim was about the loan I made to Combs, and the act of generosity and love I showed him. I fulfilled my obligation and wanted him to fulfill his end of the bargain.

Montandon's deal for Combs fell out of escrow in July 2016. Two months later, in September, he found another buyer, and I, of course, renewed my commission claim. Again, Combs denied I had any stake. Again, I sent my claim to the title company that was handling the escrow, Nevada Title.

Every time I put in a commission demand, he used his attorney, Mark Peplowski, to ferociously attack me.

Around this same time, Combs reached out to me on the phone. He wanted me to come over and "work this out." No way. I started thinking of all the coincidences around my car wreck, and I knew I would not go to his house. I was getting an unsettling vibe. I told him I had honored my end of the agreement by making the loan, and I wanted him to hold up his end of the deal.

The second time Combs' properties went into escrow, they closed—to the tune of roughly $23 million. I was certainly not going to let my share of the commission go without a fight, and I certainly wasn't going to lie down and roll over when Combs filed the suit. We had a clear oral agreement. It was a valid contract, whether it was a signed piece of paper or not. I had performed on my end of the contract, which demonstrated validity to the agreement. When the pig farm closed, I did get my loan paid back.

It was while we were in litigation that I found out Bob Combs bought pigs with the money, and they had all died from a virus. Now I knew why he relentlessly wanted me to convert to a livestock loan. Could this have possibly led to an assassination attempt on my life?

It was after my deposition regarding the pig farm commission dispute—and we were going to be deposing Montandon next—that Bob Combs' attorney Byron asked me if I knew who I was messing with. I felt it was a very strange question, and a threat. During the deposition, Combs' attorney asked about my car wreck, and I got a strange feeling that he knew who was behind it. That he knew something that I did not.

I immediately thought of Travis taunting me about my neck, about how Bob Combs bought pigs with the money I had loaned him, and how they had died, and his relentless pursuit for me to convert the loan to a livestock loan. *Yes*, I was thinking to myself, *he is one of the ones who is tied to my car wreck.*

After the depositions, we went to mediation, and Combs agreed to pay me $50,000. One huge point in my favor was the strange business of how they were trying to mess with the recordings of the transactions—a major violation of federal law. The judge said they had defamed me. They tried to accuse me of the criminal acts they were committing against me. When I countersued them for those acts, they immediately became very nervous.

The judge in the mediation even said I had a case against them, as well as Mark Peplowski, for defamation.

Combs did not exactly associate himself with the best and brightest, especially when it came to lawyers. Mark Peplowski ended up becoming a defendant in the Combs case when I countersued him.

In addition to being a lawyer, Mark Peplowski was a professor in the Department of Social Sciences at the College of Southern Nevada Henderson campus. He started part-time there in 1995 and became a full-time employee in August 2001. He earned tenure in March 2006.

Only a few months later, college administrators moved to fire him, according to the *Las Vegas Review-Journal*, after he was arrested and charged with soliciting a prostitute. He was booked on June 24, 2006. Las Vegas police officers were conducting a sting, and they witnessed a prostitute get into Peplowski's car and leave with $50. The woman told police the money was payment for a sex act.

This wasn't his last shining moment.

In 2017, shortly after Peplowski sued and defamed me on behalf of his client, Bob Combs, Peplowski faced two counts of open or gross lewdness, a gross misdemeanor offense, in connection with two separate incidents earlier in the same year. According to the *Review-Journal*, the criminal complaint (filed December 7) alleged that Peplowski engaged in sexual conduct in a public location on June 8 and again on July 19.

The newspaper said the tip about Peplowski's fondness for prostitutes came from a Clark County inmate, and that led to Peplowski being followed by police. Both incidents were allegedly captured on camera. The inmate also claimed the lawyer/professor and a prostitute were involved in criminal activity involving fraud/identity theft.

Police records would later show that Peplowski picked up a woman on June 8, 2017, in his gold Toyota Highlander, and had sex with her as they stood outside the vehicle in a vacant lot. On July 19, 2017, Peplowski allegedly picked up a different woman in the 2500 block of Fremont Street in Downtown Las Vegas. He had been roaming an area where prostitution is known to occur.

Peplowski's attorney argued that police had to use "high-powered binoculars" to view these incidents, which nullified the arrests. His attorney claimed the use of binoculars was like someone using a high-powered telescope to peer into a bedroom window.

The charges were dropped. Peplowski stopped working for the college in the summer of 2016, but it's still not clear if he resigned or was fired.

When Peplowksi was arrested, it felt as if God was protecting me from a horrible human being.

It was in March of 2017, while I was working out at Lifetime Fitness in Summerlin, that I felt an overwhelming fear for my life. I glanced across the gym and a humungous human being was lifting weights that seemed familiar. He was not looking at me, but I could tell he was radiating this really dark energy. I felt like my life was at stake. It was time for me to hightail it out of there. The second I left, Mordred called me up and said Mike Levin just saw you at the gym. This told me my assistant was friends with a very dangerous person. Days later, his father and Mordred went into escrow with Mike Levin on a piece of land at Craig and Allen through my brokerage behind my back—where Mike Levin would get 10% ownership of the property and is the broker for the buyer. This was the same thing he proposed to Farbod when I kicked him out of Farbod's house and wanted Farbod to buy property. The buyer was getting the earnest money back after 30 days and keeping the escrow open with no earnest money down! How was this negotiated with one of the shrewdest buyers in the Las Vegas Valley? I felt an overwhelming sensation that this was payback for my wreck. I disputed Mike Levin's buyer getting his earnest money back. Mike Levin negotiated with my client without me, and so I disputed the earnest money release. Through extensions, Farbod ended up keeping his earnest money. Mike Levin's hatred for me was intense. I also had a quiet satisfaction telling myself, *well the murder attempt failed, and you lost your deposit*. I felt he was somehow connected to my death. When I was dealing with Mike Levin, he acted like he knew something I did not. It was as if Mike did something horrible to me, and he was taunting me about it. Mike Levin referred to me as Mikey and claimed he was also part of the Sattari family like me. Levin tried to get me to sign on an extension of the escrow on behalf of Farbod, trying to get me to perform an illegal act. I ended up blocking him from contacting me. I did not need Mike Levin in my life, especially when that person threw off such darkness. I love how Mike Levin lost his client's earnest money as well. It showed the Karma that existed in the universe.

The experience left me profoundly shaken. Why did Farbod go into escrow on his property where the buyer gets his earnest money back and the escrow is still open? Why did he do these things behind my back? I had a profound feeling that they were all tied to the murder attempt on my life. I could not let the Sattaris know. I had to continue letting things play out. I did not have all the answers yet.

CHAPTER 19

In Search of Medical Answers

L et's return to my medical recovery and, for that, we need to go back to late spring of 2016—the time when I was wasting away and feeling deeply vulnerable.

Before the wreck, I was a person who was afraid of growing old and dying. I wanted to live forever. After the wreck, all I wanted to do was die. I knew something was seriously wrong. Why did I feel like this? Would the feeling last? And for how long?

I became extremely sensitive to everything in the universe. Lights. Noises. Bad people. Before the wreck, I trained in mixed martial arts. I was a badass. After the wreck, I wasn't so sure of myself. I lost that confidence I'd always had. I also noticed that certain people in life were throwing off the uncontrollable willies.

The official definition of "willies" is "a strong feeling of nervous apprehension and discomfort." To me, it's a chill. The hairs on the back of my neck stand up. The chill goes down my spine. Whenever the willies happened on a profound scale, it felt like when I died and the universe judged me.

Why did Nahid, Mordred, and Farbod Sattari now all throw off the willies? Why did Travis Nelson, the marketing representative for Nevada Title, throw off the willies? Numerous others too. I was even getting the willies around Mike Gonzales, who was a longtime friend.

It was as if they all knew something I did not. I told myself that I was crazy to imagine these things. Yet something in my essence had changed. I felt more aware of my surroundings, and I realized I now saw things differently than most people. It felt as if old parts of my brain were no longer getting blood and new parts of it were.

I had been hit so violently, I ended up in the afterlife and came back, never losing consciousness—but why couldn't I move on? That was all I wanted to do: get my commission from the pig farm and Hualapai and Farm, fire the Sattari family, and move on.

I never suffered from depression before the car crash. But after the wreck, it seemed I was constantly going through the experience over and over in my mind. It was like a hundred car wrecks all at once. I always felt as if the collision happened one second ago, and this put me on edge. Time was not helping me gain any perspective or distance from the event itself.

The anxiety started slowly suffocating me. It eventually trickled into depression. It is hard to feel anxiety all the time *without* it trickling into depression. Depression and anxiety go hand in hand. I never thought of taking my life before the car wreck. After the wreck, it seemed like a viable option and something I considered regularly.

During the first months after the incident, I felt closed-in, reclusive, and sad. Through my own research, I knew this was because of a traumatic brain injury. I also knew the suicide rate for those who suffered traumatic brain injuries was through the roof.

It was in these dark times when I had an overwhelming feeling about killing myself. I did not understand why I would have been allowed to survive, when I felt so awful after returning to the physical universe. What was even more startling was my inability to sleep. The viscous assault on my life was a constant companion that never seemed to ebb with time. I would go to sleep around 9:00 p.m. and then wake up minutes later—fully awake.

Suicide became something I thought of regularly, where before it was not something I would ever consider doing. For the first time ever, I was truly depressed and knew I had to do something about it if I was to live. It was during these dark times I decided to kill myself and then was shown the vision of hell by God.

. . . .

I finally reached out to my primary caregiver, Dr. Mitchell Phillips, about a month after the wreck, in March 2016.

I knew something was seriously wrong. I needed help. I had been Dr. Phillips' patient since 2003 and had referred dozens of people to his practice over the years. I was an exceptional patient and brought him lots of business.

The first person I saw at Dr. Phillips' office was a nurse practitioner named Julie. She wanted to see if my neck had been broken. I didn't tell Julie or anyone about my consciousness leaving my body.

But Julie didn't find anything. I went home feeling nothing was accomplished, but I made another appointment at Dr. Phillips' clinic. The next time, I was crying. I felt like I was in a coffin and couldn't get out.

On this second visit, I saw Doug Turner. He's an EMT who had joined the Army Rangers in 1984 and trained as a Special Forces Combat Medic. Through the army, he received his BS from the University of Oklahoma and his Masters in Family Practice from the University of Nebraska. Doug had vast experience in sports medicine, orthopedics, and pain management. Doug had real worry in his eyes. He was the first medical professional to express true concern while evaluating me for a diagnosis.

Still, I did not get any help for my brain. I returned a third time to Dr. Phillips' office and was tearful once again. I felt I was becoming a character in Stephen King's book *Thinner*. My blood pressure was through the roof, like I'd just run a marathon. *Not good!*

Dr. Phillips told me to quit sobbing. He said that if I did not quit crying, he would put in my medical record that I was faking it.

I quit crying and immediately became angry. I was obviously hurt, and Dr. Phillips wanted to make my injury about me getting a paycheck. I was flabbergasted. If my motive was money from the wreck, I would have gone to the emergency room right after the collision.

I finally figured out that what I was dealing with had to be connected to my brain. "What's going on with me is brain-related," I said. "I want a referral to a neurologist."

He gave me a list of neurologists but told me no referral was needed. I was welcome to call and schedule an appointment, and they would get me in.

I thanked him for the list of neurologists, but I was still in shock—and angry—that he threatened me over being emotional. The last thing I ever wanted to be diagnosed with was a traumatic brain injury (TBI).

I couldn't care less about any litigation. It was about getting help for something I knew was serious.

I went home and called all the neurologists. I found out none of them would see me without a referral from my primary care doctor. I couldn't believe it!

I called Dr. Phillips' office, but they would not give me the referral. They wanted me to come back and schedule another appointment to get one. This was ridiculous, as I had asked Dr. Phillips directly for the referral the last time I was there. Plus, at the last appointment, they were several hours late to see me. I thought to myself: *What a horrific doctor. Why do I need this guy in my life?*

I fired Dr. Mitchell Phillips. I no longer wanted to see him—ever. How dare he threaten me? The last thing I wanted in my life was a Godless human with a God complex. I was deeply offended by his treatment of me.

I engaged a legal firm, Ganz and Hauf. They were referred to me by the bishop of the Mormon Church in my ward. I did not go to church often but did visit the Mormon church a few times. This was at the beginning of April, six or seven weeks after the wreck. I reached out to the bishop when I found out I must have been seriously hurt.

When I could not get in to see a neurologist, I panicked. With no help from Dr. Phillips, I finally got in to see a neurologist named Dr. Aury Nagy. I knew from our very first meeting that Dr. Nagy was a good person. He put me in physical therapy and started treating me. He did not allow me to exercise or do my martial arts, which was a disturbing thing to have taken from my regular routine, but it felt good to have a plan, and it felt good to have a doctor who listened to me.

When I started getting treatment, I found out that the litigation game can become just as vicious as commercial real estate. Doctors take sides, whether they are for the patient or for the insurance company. I could not believe it. Shouldn't everyone be there for the patient?

The first thing I needed to get help for was my overwhelming depression and despair. I knew I wouldn't live much longer if that wasn't fixed. The idea of killing myself was overwhelming.

I was in a very dark place. I did not know the long-term ramifications of what was done to me. All I thought about was how eternally at peace I would be when I was deceased. I had a profound anxiety that was ever-present. I would compare it to being buried alive in a coffin.

Dr. Nagy referred me to a neuropsychologist by the name of Dr. Staci Johnson. I liked her immediately. She was a year younger and a business owner, like me. I loved all her tattoos. I also thought she was quite attractive and developed a little crush on her.

She gave me an exam to see how the wreck impacted me. She diagnosed me with PTSD. She determined, however, that it was psychosomatic. In other words, she concluded, it was a physical illness caused or aggravated by a mental factor such as internal conflict or stress. Other doctors disagreed with her on this point, however.

Who wants a brain injury with *physical* damage? Not me.

I was a top producer in the land game in Clark County. Again, the last thing I wanted was a traumatic brain injury showing physical damage. I loved her diagnosis of the PTSD being psychosomatic. I was hopeful it was true. Why? Because I did not want any physical damage. Of course! I also couldn't care less about litigation. I just wanted to find the will to live again.

I started seeing Dr. Johnson on a regular basis. We talked about my depression and anxiety. For a while, she seemed to help me. During our first meeting, I told her I was not sleeping on the damaged side. She started looking at my MRI and saw the damage done to the right side of my brain. She asked me to sleep on the damaged side to see what would happen. I did, and it caused headaches. The fact that she was having me sleep on the injured side showed that she saw the damage in the MRI herself and was practicing out of her area of expertise. It also told me that her psychosomatic report was bullshit.

I enjoyed some of my sessions with Staci Johnson, and I enjoyed some of her insight into my injury. I could tell she saw many cases, from the most extreme to the least extreme. She had Mordred fill out a questionnaire asking if I changed at all after the car wreck. Mordred answered that I did not act the same around him afterward. I never had the feeling of the willies before I died. After I died, this feeling became overwhelming around him.

Dr. Nagy also wanted me to see a neurologist, but it was hard to see anyone because no one wanted to get involved in litigation. It was my new primary care doctor, Dr. Ramanathan of Doctors of Green Valley, who referred me to the neurologist who saved my life.

That neurologist was Dr. Enrico Fazzini. When I first saw him, he seemed a little standoffish, as if he was super busy. I had the sense that he didn't think I needed to be there. Perhaps he thought I appeared to be fully functioning, so why was I here?

I told Dr. Fazzini about the wreck, and that I hadn't felt the same since it happened. I told him about a constant crazy pressure on the right side of my skull that was always there. He immediately wanted to refer me to SimonMed, a medical imaging facility, for a special and more advanced MRI. I thanked Dr. Fazzini profusely. Finally, I had found a neurologist who could treat me. This was in October 2016 (right around the time of the second meeting at the Oasis RV Park). It had taken nearly eight months of bouncing around clinics and doctors' offices to find the right professional.

The next time I had therapy with Dr. Johnson, I told her about my new neurologist and my MRI. She immediately started bad-mouthing Dr. Fazzini. She said he was a good doctor, but "only if you want a good court case."

I was angered by how she bad-mouthed Dr. Fazzini. It was like pulling teeth to just get a neurologist to treat me, and then when I found one, Dr. Johnson attacked him.

Dr. Fazzini was there to help me. When I tried to contact other neurologists, they would not treat me because they did not want to be in any possible litigation. What was Dr. Johnson talking about? I was battling depression and the will to live. Why would I give a rat's ass about a lawsuit? I made my own money and did not get ahead by suing people. I did it through hard work and going above and beyond for my clients. I felt there was no chance of getting a decent settlement anyway, as I waited over a month to go see a doctor.

Dr. Johnson tried to talk to me about getting the MRI. I told her I wanted the analysis because I wanted to see what damage was done to my brain.

However, she also wanted me to agree that if the results came back as "normal," I would not sue.

"I need to see how this injury is impacting me in this life," I thought. "I am not getting the answers from you and others that I was seeking. On the contrary, it seems like every doctor, apart from a couple, are doing everything in their power to cover up how this injury is going to impact me and my future."

I agreed with Dr Johnson to get rid of my litigation if the SimonMed MRI came back normal.

I went in for the MRI and did what I was told to do—remain still for forty minutes while the machine did its work. Talk about being buried alive in a coffin; that's what an MRI is like while you're trying to lie still in a confined tube.

I was not supposed to look at the results without Dr. Johnson. But I had a crazy pressure headache one night, and I realized I couldn't wait until my appointment with her, which was a couple of weeks away from that point.

I picked up the results and went to see a longtime friend of mine by the name of Dr. Randy Birdman. I got to know him two decades before, when I was cold-calling expired listings. He had a multimillion-dollar home for sale for which a listing had expired when I first called him to offer my help.

I took the MRI readings to Dr. Birdman's house, and we reviewed the results together. They were horrific, to say the least.

I called Dr. Johnson and left her a message, saying that I went over the results with a doctor friend of mine and how frightening they were. Dr. Johnson also had a copy of the findings and called me on the phone. She told me not to panic, and when I later met with her at my scheduled appointment, she made a big point of emphasizing one thing:

"Don't ever let anyone tell you these turn into brain-wasting injuries," she said. Those words gave me that paralyzing fear again. I thought her comment was bizarre. She also told me I would have to start vocalizing my thoughts to remember things and that I would suffer from cognitive brain fatigue. She was a psychologist; how could she know all these things?

When I went over the results with Dr. Fazzini, he told me he had seen thousands of brain injuries and that I was in the top 1 to 2 percent in terms of how badly my brain had been physically damaged.

Dr. Fazzini was immediately concerned for my health. He gave me his cell phone number and personal email address. I felt relieved. I had a good person looking out for me at last. I asked Dr. Fazzini how much time I had left on this earth, and he said he would give me twenty years tops.

"*Twenty years?*" I exclaimed. "I'm only forty-six years old."

"Then maybe a few more years than that," he said.

I realized he was softening his language so I would not start panicking.

Dr. Fazzini also told me that he was recently in court where he and Dr. Johnson shared a patient; Dr. Johnson tried to claim that cases like mine don't turn into brain-wasting injuries. That's exactly what she had told me.

In my meeting with Dr. Johnson to go over my MRI results, she got on the phone with her assistant to get me in—as soon as possible— to see a speech therapist named Theresa Stempien. Speech therapists often are asked to see patients with major brain damage. She then told me good luck with my litigation. Yikes, she was acknowledging the seriousness of my injury and no longer asking me to settle.

I got in to see Stempien immediately and told her I was prescribed medical cannabis for my injury. She grinned from ear to ear and began to interrogate me for several hours. It was like a deposition. At the end of the long questioning session, she finally told me she couldn't treat me because I had used cannabis in the past. I realized she was trying to create a report for the defense—if there was to be any future litigation.

When I asked her about my wreck she replied, "Don't worry about that—that was just like you were getting shaken around like a little baby."

I contained my anger. I clearly saw her trying to provoke me to make my entire car wreck about some bullshit squabble.

The creep factor with Theresa Stempien went through the roof. My PTSD was going off. She was throwing off the uncontrollable willies.

I would soon come to realize that what was going on was actually my amplified intuition. Somehow, the part of my brain that was hurt was allowing me to perceive people for their true nature.

After the interview, Stempien started texting me at inappropriate hours, asking me super personal questions. That was when I fired her.

"You're not allowed to fire me," she said.

I told her to invoice me, and I would pay her whatever I owed, but we were finished. She sent me her report, which I gave to my attorney unopened. My attorneys told me she rendered a report on me using cannabis and not the actual wreck. That may have worked in the Reagan era; legalization of cannabis was only months away in Nevada.

She started engaging and nagging my insurance company, and she sent me a report about my condition. I have never opened it. I will never read it. I did not want her to trigger my PTSD. Her opinion of me was of such little concern that I would not allow her to enter my life and start harassing me. She was inconsequential to me. I felt that her only job on this earth was trying to hurt others and jump into their litigation, trying to create an argument for the defense.

I told Dr. Johnson about her "friend's" behavior. Dr. Johnson had Stempien's report in front of her. There was a big shit-eating grin on Dr. Johnson's face.

"I am not here to talk about your creepy friend," I said. "I am here to battle my depression and find a will to live. I have blocked your friend from contacting me, and I refuse to open her report. I couldn't care less what her opinion is of me."

"Are you always going to block people who make you feel uncomfortable?" she said.

"It works for me," I said.

Every time I met with Dr Johnson after that, she would always bring up Theresa Stempien and comment that she didn't agree with her report. I would respond that I was sure if I read it, I would also not agree.

I was not going to read it. Ever. Why would I? I had too much going on in my life just trying to find the will to live again. Why would I let someone aggravate me, especially someone who was not even a doctor? Theresa was nothing to me and was removed from my life when I blocked her from contacting me on my cell phone.

CHAPTER 20

Medical Recovery

W hat I needed was some answers. How was the injury impacting me? Affecting me? What were the risks? What could I do to get better? Why was I getting these awful headaches?

I wasn't getting the answers I needed.

And more important to me than anything, why was it that certain people were throwing off the willies?

I reached out to Dr. Fazzini, and he gave me a referral that saved my life. He referred me to NCEP, the nonprofit that treats people with brain injuries. NCEP was just what I needed.

I told Dr. Johnson about NCEP and she tried, aggressively, to talk me out of getting involved with the organization. She thought many people being treated at NCEP couldn't function as well as I did, and she didn't think the organization was a good fit for me.

Why was this lady so concerned with my treatment? So dismissive?

I interviewed with Dawn Zito, the admissions coordinator at NCEP. I told her about my dramatic weight loss. She made an "*ewww*" sound and then informed me that this indicated the most serious kind of brain injury.

Dawn Zito agreed to admit me as a client in late October 2016.

I mentioned to Dr. Johnson that I couldn't wait to get seen and learn how to deal with my injury. I knew her client was not really me but the insurance company she billed. If I stopped seeing Dr. Johnson, she would earn less money. She would also not be able to downplay the significance of my injury to my insurance company.

By January, however, I had heard nothing about getting started at NCEP. I reached out to Dawn Zito. Dawn emailed me a letter that stated after talking to my attorney and Dr. Johnson, they determined I did not need to be admitted to NCEP. I found out that Dr. Johnson talked NCEP out of admitting me *after they had already agreed to take me in!*

I could not believe she interfered with my treatment! I complained to Dr. Fazzini, who raised holy hell with NCEP, insisting that they admit me. He told them my physical damage was quite severe, even if I was functioning better than most.

Dr. Fazzini's pressure worked. The next time back at NCEP, I was interviewed by NCEP director Jerry Kaeppler. This time, the interview lasted for several hours. Kaeppler, who was once a boxer in college, could tell I was horribly distraught. I told him I felt very alone with my injury. He was empathetic to my situation, in part, because he once got knocked out during a boxing match and never slept well again. He told me that brain injuries will amplify what we already have going on inside us. I had slight attention deficit disorder before the car wreck; I had major ADD after. I was a little lonely before the car wreck, but felt much more prolonged feelings of loneliness after. I was intuitive before the car wreck; I had Godlike levels of intuition after. Some people call that PTSD. I found out through NCEP that it is intuition amplified.

Kaeppler agreed to take me in as a patient. I told him that ever since the wreck, I could not look over my right shoulder due to the pain. He introduced me to a great massage therapist, Michelle Viesselman. She snapped my neck back in place for the first time since the wreck. Driving home that day, I looked over my right shoulder to check on traffic, and for the first time since everything happened, I had no pain in my neck.

When I confessed my near-death experience and everything surrounding it, Jerry Kaeppler exclaimed that what happened to me was special. That I was touched by God.

After learning that Dr. Johnson was interfering with my treatment, I fired her. Who wouldn't?

The other major change—and this plays a big role in my investigation, in my effort to find the bridge—was that I started to understand more about the times I would get the willies around certain people.

When I began working with NCEP I learned that when you have PTSD, the chills are essentially a super intense "spider sense." It also alerts animals of a dangerous human or helps them anticipate an earthquake.

As a patient, and then later becoming a volunteer at NCEP, I learned that anxiety and excitement are the same emotion; they are essentially two sides of the same coin. It's a matter of how you view your life. It's whether you view life positively or negatively. It's the proverbial question, is the glass half empty or half full? When I learned this little tidbit, I never suffered from depression quite the same way again. I will get that feeling from time to time, but it's not as intense. Before this information, I would drive to work with a feeling of such profound anxiety I would sometimes cry in my car. Now, when something causes anxiety, I try to view it more as excitement. Today, the feeling of being in a coffin is not like it was before. They gave me a new outlook on life. I give all the credit to NCEP. Without them, suicide would have seemed like a viable option to my dilemma.

One of the other things I learned at NCEP was that brain injuries are based on how well you function. They are not based on the physical damage to the brain itself. You can have an MRI show very little damage yet if that person does not function, they are considered as having a severe traumatic brain injury. My doctor and others said they never saw people function at my level with such a bad MRI. As a result, my injury was categorized as mild to moderate, not sever. And the top 20 percent of brain injuries with the most severe physical damage often lead to the brain's wasting away—and death—over time.

Dr. Fazzini had said I was in the top 1 to 2 percent. And then I realized Dr. Johnson's comments to me the second she saw my SimonMed MRI results: "Don't let anyone tell you these turn into brain-wasting injuries."

Why would she have said that to me, especially when I was seeing her for depression? That did not help with my depression at all. In fact, it had the opposite effect on my treatment, as I then felt very frightened.

NCEP allowed me to see my injury, not for how horrible it was, but how blessed I was to have survived, and to be able to move on at my own level. I went from life to death, back to life, never losing consciousness or spending time in a coma.

It was an almost unheard-of experience on this earth.

. . . .

At NCEP, I noticed the patients did not have a TV to view videos. The instructors used little iPads for a big class. I bought NCEP a big-screen TV. Nothing made me prouder than when I would walk by the TV Room and see all the people watching the TV I had purchased. The next thing I noticed, was that NCEP needed a bed. The only bed they had looked like it belonged in an old hospital from the 1970s. It was beyond nasty. When you suffer from a severe concussion, one of the possible side effects is you do not get enough sleep, or you get too much sleep. I bought NCEP a bed and box spring. I was very proud to be around a bunch of people who cared for me and were concerned about my health, so I wanted to do something for them. Finally, I had people who cared about my well-being—and not any possible litigation.

I graduated from NCEP in April 2017, fourteen months after the wreck. There is always a big ceremony for those graduating from NCEP. It was very emotional, and when they asked me to speak in front of all the patients and staff, I was weeping and found it hard to get one word out.

. . . .

Right away, I became part of NCEP's work program and then became a volunteer. I still battled depression. All the work gave me special insight into others dealing with traumatic brain injuries.

I had a change of heart about seeing Dr. Johnson. I needed somebody to talk to about depression. I had learned how fortunate I was to be able to walk and talk and be fully functional. I still made a better living than most people. And if I was depressed, then I was not viewing life the proper way. In other words, I had learned that attitude is everything.

Right before my first meeting with Dr. Johnson, before I moved on to another psychologist, her assistant always called me at inappropriate hours, usually between 8:00 and 10:00 p.m. One of the things I learned at NCEP was that if you have a traumatic brain injury, some people will try to take advantage of you. The late-evening calls were strange, and my enhanced intuition told me she was trying to trigger my PTSD.

I had also told Dr. Johnson, before I fired her, that I usually went to bed early. And I told her that with my head injury and PTSD diagnosis, I didn't like receiving such extreme late-night phone calls from her assistant at such inappropriate hours.

After I reached out to reconnect with Dr. Johnson, her assistant called me on Good Friday; it was late at night. She claimed I had called her earlier in the day, trying to reschedule an appointment with Dr. Johnson. I had done no such thing. I realized right then and there, because of the physical damage done to my brain, that her assistant was trying to take advantage of me.

I felt Dr. Johnson was trying to make my potential litigation about me not getting along with her assistant. After the strange call on Good Friday, I met with Dr. Johnson one more time, but I didn't like my feeling about her at all. She was triggering my PTSD. She was changing the subject when I tried to talk to her about her assistant's behavior. I knew I would not be seeing her again.

I could not help myself. I wanted to share one thing I had learned at NCEP—that brain injury patients who are treated with THC and CBD recover at a much faster rate, which is why they believed I was functioning so well.

I could see the anger flash in Dr. Johnson's eyes. It appeared she had taken great trouble to sabotage my case by sending me to Theresa Stempien, the speech therapist, who wanted to make the case about me being treated with cannabis—and now I had one of the biggest nonprofit caregivers of this type of injury backing me, teaching me how it could impact my life. NCEP even said it was fine for me to use cannabis.

At NCEP, I was working in the machine shop with people who had lost the ability to be mechanics. We were making cuckoo clocks, and the equipment was very loud. Beyond loud. It was almost painful. The injury had left me extremely hypersensitive to the universe, noises, and certain people.

And, in my opinion, this sensitivity allowed me to solve my own death.

I was given a second ability to perceive. I could see with my eyes, of course. But my whole body would react to the people around me. It's a very acute feeling. It's an enhancement of intuition—to an extreme level.

It helped me realize why I would get the willies when I was around Mordred, Nahid, and Farbod. And why I would get the willies around Bob Combs.

I had never noticed it before the wreck. But now everything seemed different with all of them.

So, let's recap a few important facts.

When the car wreck happened, I was in shock. I was dazed. I had just gone to my Maker and come back. I was fighting with the voice of God. But I didn't know I was suffering from a severe concussion. I was still functioning, so I found a way to ignore what I was feeling at the time.

I had the confrontation with the driver where he wanted me to commit insurance fraud and say I was moving, even though I was fully braked.

There were no skid marks at the four-way stop. I had heard no braking noise.

When I didn't agree to the insurance fraud, the driver got violently confrontational with me—*screaming* at me. The shiver of death went down my spine.

I knew I had only survived because Robert Drysdale had me do neck crunches in preparation for my blue belt in jiu-jitsu. My belt test was going to be the Saturday after the Wednesday when my car wreck happened.

I left the wreck for the meeting with my attorney, where I had been heading before my death.

My attorney saw my frazzled state, and Gloria Setoni, his paralegal, wanted me to go to the ER. Immediately. I refused. Then my attorney sent me to collect various documents—bank statements and things like that—as part of the pending IRS audit of my company's 401(k).

I drove around town and gathered what they needed. It seemed like a doable task, but of course, I was traumatized. I couldn't shake the feeling that the wreck had just happened a second ago—a feeling that would last for years and years. In fact, to this day.

I had the driver's insurance information, and I had a picture of the damage to the bumper on his truck, but that day, in that moment, my plan was to move on with my life. I knew I was rattled, but I had no idea how badly.

I knew I would have to call my insurance company at some point, but I put that to the side and went about my day. The audit I was going through for my company's 401(k) seemed to be more pressing. I was fighting with God too. I wanted to move on. I wanted to pretend none of this shit had just happened. But I had no idea how seriously hurt I was at the time.

It wasn't until later that night that I realized I had forgotten to do something important.

And it finally came back to me—the entire car wreck. The whole moment came rushing back. I felt a rush of tears and emotion. How could I have forgotten it?

If you research brain injuries, you'll see it's a very common experience. I was really hurt. I believe I had a brain bleed, but on the outside I looked normal. I knew something was seriously wrong with me that first night and many nights since because I'd only sleep for a couple minutes. I was like, "Why do I have this weird anxiety feeling? How come I'm not sleeping?"

Star, my dog, came to sleep next to me in bed—very unusual. She became a third pillow, sleeping right by her dad's head. Before the wreck, she would sleep next to my bed, not in my bed. She also sensed something was very wrong.

That first night, somewhere between being awake and asleep, I heard a very loud whisper:

Your life will never be the same.

I immediately sat up startled; *did I just hear that?* The whisper sounded so close and yet so far away—but I did hear it.

That voice at night was the second supernatural voice I had heard in one day, the first being the voice of God.

If God was correct that the wreck was an attempted assassination, then it had failed. I was going to stick around, get my commission from Farbod Sattari for Hualapai and Farm, and get the hell out of the relationship with the Sattaris if they had anything to do with my attempted murder.

My health was slowly deteriorating, and I was losing a tremendous amount of weight. The coincidences were startling. But I still needed to see things play out.

If I could feel better, I would move on with my life. I would forget about the crazy experience of dying, and I would just move on.

But one thing was for sure—I was not going to leave the Sattari family until I found out the truth.

I was going into serious investigation mode.

CHAPTER 21

Moments of Clarity

B ack in the world of real estate, where I was, of course, plugging along and doing what I could to pull deals together—I could no longer deal with Farbod when it came to negotiating offers. I asked Mordred to review proposals with Farbod. Farbod's personality seemed to have changed—he wasn't acting quite as crazy toward me as he was before. Nonetheless, I didn't want to risk being around him when he might blow up, so I used Mordred as the go-between. Farbod's yelling was hard for me to handle with my new sensitivity to the universe.

Farbod, Mordred, and Nahid, as I've mentioned, were all throwing off a chill. Here were three people that I had always loved and cared about, and now, I could no longer stand their presence. I did not feel safe around them anymore.

Farbod called me regularly to tell me how much Ray Ghouli was bad-mouthing me toward the end of our relationship before I fired him as a client. He also would regularly tell me that Mordred would never cause me any physical harm. Why was he saying these things to me? I would put it out of my mind, as it gave me the chills every time he called me.

I noticed that certain people's demeanor changed around me. Not just with the Sattaris, but also with my officemate agents, Mike Gonzales and George Greiner. With Mike, at first, it was his overall attitude and then a few coincidences with people that I felt were involved in my wreck. Mike was writing offers for Jim Zeiter where they were dictating what commissions my brokerage was going to make on a deal. Mike also went into escrow with Farbod behind my back on a property I showed to Mike that Farbod owned. He went into escrow behind my back and then tried to dictate that I would only make 20% of the commission on the deal, when I was the one who put it together. The deal never closed. It threw off the creeps when this went down. I was the broker, and I was the only one who had a say on my commission, not my agents.

George left my company a year after the murder attempt. Right before he left, he confided in me that he got himself kicked out of the Navy by saying he was gay when he really wasn't. When he told me this story, I wanted him gone from my brokerage. I have a family member who was gay that served 30 years in the military. After he left, he would have someone call me on a regular basis asking for George. It was like he was trying to keep tabs on me.

At the same time, Mordred had a hard time putting offers in front of Farbod.

In June 2017, Mordred went into an uncontrolled rage in my office. He smashed his father's paintings in my conference room. He was in a violent fight with his own father over the phone. What a mess—and what a mess of a family. Farbod was causing his own son to have a nervous breakdown.

The explosive yelling by both father and son reminded me of the times he would say people came by the office looking for me. Mordred claimed these people, whoever they were, would slap him around. When I questioned him about this, he would become angry and hysterical toward me.

Who needed to deal with this shit? This behavior? Not me! I had never seen such rage coming from a human being, except from Mordred's father. Farbod and Mordred were ingrained into my real estate company, and they inserted themselves into my car wreck litigation as my top witnesses, but I still wanted to see if I could find a way to get my commission on Hualapai and Farm. I did not care about my car wreck litigation; I cared about the deals I was to broker. It gave off the creeps like no other when they would insist on being in my litigation.

Nonetheless, I felt uncomfortable and afraid for my life. *How could such violent people not be behind my near-death experience?* I was digging in my heels; I would not go anywhere until I found out the truth and got paid on Hualapai and Farm!

I had just paid Nahid and Mordred close to $50,000 on a commission they did not earn. One thing I would do for sure, once I put Hualapai and Farm in escrow and it closed, I would fire Farbod Sattari.

· · · ·

I got a call from Nahid after Mordred's breakdown in my office. She told me that Farbod had started yelling at Mordred and that he no longer treated him like a human being. She then said Farbod is treating Mordred like me. I did not like all of this violence between Farbod and Mordred. Now, with Nahid's call, I had confirmation of Farbod's explosive tendencies and what he truly thought about me.

With all this drama, my guard was up.

Around June 2017, Mordred came to me and said his parents wanted him to move out of their house and move in with me.

No way, José.

Farbod tried to talk me into the idea on the phone. I laughed. Farbod could tell his pleas were falling on deaf ears.

Mordred? The guy who had long claimed that people would assault him because they were looking for me? Why would I let him live in my house? Why would I let all the Sattari drama into my home, especially with my fears about the car wreck and the connection to the Sattaris? Especially after what my lord Elohim told me.

It wasn't going to happen.

I told Farbod that Mordred was going to need to find his own way in life. I told him it was not my responsibility to look after his kids. Farbod became infuriated, but my intuition was going through the roof. If

Mordred was behind my car wreck, in any way, then living with me would give him the perfect opportunity to try and murder me for a second time.

I noticed right after the wreck, for some reason, that Mordred stopped mentioning that people were looking for me—people who, he claimed, would slap him around when he said he didn't know where I was. I wasn't being taunted about this anymore for some reason. How could people go through life slapping Mordred around like some silly bitch? And now all the silly bitch-slapping stops once I get violently hurt? This was all ridiculous.

In a rather creepy fashion, Mordred started asking me a question:

"What would you do if somebody broke into your house while you were sleeping?" He asked this on multiple occasions.

Mordred asked it with a disturbing giggle. With Mordred, the creep factor was through the roof—at an astronomical level. Before I died, I loved and cared about Mordred and all the Sattaris, but something had changed. I never saw him, his father, or his mother in the same light again.

They all threw off the chill of death.

Farbod started calling me up on a nightly basis, claiming that his son would never cause me any bodily harm. He also said he wanted to get involved in the lawsuit over the car wreck. Farbod pursued being a character witness—he pursued this hard, the same fanatical way I went after land deals.

All Farbod would ever mention was how he was going to be the best witness in the world for my car wreck. I thought it was bizarre. I had tried to downplay the crash and had not asked him to do any such thing on my behalf.

"Mike, I'll be your number one witness," said Farbod. Over and over.

He had never asked what happened to me after the wreck! He had never asked about the details of what had happened. I told him I was in a car wreck, and I believed I had suffered a concussion. Apparently, that was enough. He did not want to know anything more. Yet he wanted to be a big part of my case.

Strange!

Mordred would tell me the same thing.

I hired a new neuropsychologist by the name of Dr. Loong. Dr. Loong would only take on the most serious cases, and when I told him what happened, he was shocked. He could not believe the driver did not use his brakes with such a massive pickup truck. He then informed me that people who go through trauma like that don't live more than seven years.

Dr. Loong wanted witnesses who knew me before and after the wreck. He contacted Mordred and Farbod. They both gave their testimony that the wreck really hurt me, and I changed. Dr. Loong said they were very good witnesses.

The moment of true clarity came two years after my death. I was with my accountant, John. It was when John started to tell me about his own near-death experience that something in me was triggered. His experience was completely different than mine. In John's case, he was having back surgery. He recalled that while he was asleep, waiting for his surgery, he had a dream about an angel who came to him and said he had a broken bone shard in his back. After the dream, the doctors told John they didn't want to do the surgery because they didn't see anything wrong. But John was insistent. The doctors went ahead with surgery and found the bone shard.

A miracle.

When John told me his story, I told him about my near-death experience. I told him about my message from God. I burst out crying when I gave him my testimony. I was no longer going to deny the voice of God.

The fog was finally lifting.

CHAPTER 22

Piecing the Puzzle Together

As I started to come out of my fog, the pieces of the puzzle began coming together.

I had a special gift in October 2017, more than eighteen months after my wreck. It was right around Halloween.

Mordred stole his real estate license off my wall and emailed me a form to sign so he could change offices. It is illegal for a licensee to take their real estate license from a broker; the license belongs with the broker. But he emailed me the form for a transfer after the license was gone.

He just left! I was relieved.

It felt like someone just took several tons of bricks off my back. *Good riddance*. I still did not have certain answers from Mordred, however. I knew God wanted me to have him in my life until I was given the answers I was looking for.

I somehow felt my business with Mordred was not concluded and stayed in touch with him after he left. I still did not have certain answers regarding my car wreck. Too much strangeness had happened, and I was relieved Mordred was gone. I was going to get my Hualapai and Farm commission and get this family out of my life. I was not going to be their lifelong broker.

That Halloween in 2017, around 10:00 p.m., there was a knock at my front door. To say it was a *knock* is an understatement. It was a forceful pounding. A paralyzing fear overtook my body. I somehow managed to fight through the paralysis and made my way upstairs with my two dogs, Laurel and Star. I knew on the other side of that door was death. I wasn't going to answer to confirm it, either.

When Mordred left and I ended up going through written discovery in 2018 is when I realized that the Sattaris—Farbod, Nahid, and Mordred, at least—had a hand in my car wreck or knew what happened to me.

Beyond a shadow of a doubt.

While I had these listings, the Sattaris forever had their hooks in me. Also, Nahid and Jessamine were both agents at my firm. I was in a very precarious situation.

I also realized during my written discovery, looking back from that moment of clarity, that Farbod, Mordred, and Nahid had been very nervous around me ever since the car wreck. I noticed that the Sattaris' behavior changed considerably, right after the car wreck.

Why?

Because I had survived.

The Sattaris had been doing strange things. I had a good friend, who was also my attorney specializing in real estate litigation, that represented me during the Combs litigation. Rather strangely, right after the car wreck, Farbod Sattari called him up and tried to hire him. According to my attorney, Farbod sounded quite nervous. The call was about a lease. They left it that Farbod would call him back and give him a copy of the lease, but he never did. Why would Farbod call up *my attorney* to engage him at that time? Was he trying to find out if I was thinking about a lawsuit over the car wreck? Or did he want to hire my attorney so he couldn't represent me if I filed a lawsuit against Farbod? The only lease I could think that Farbod might have a question about was the lease he had with me on the office building. Farbod Sattari didn't have leases other than mine and the beach house he owned; he was a landowner. Farbod ended up befriending another partner at the law firm. It was beyond strange to listen to Farbod talk about his blooming relationship with this guy.

I realized that the Sattaris had been creepy after the wreck. That made me more guarded. The shell-shock syndrome (PTSD) made me very reclusive. I didn't work as much because my heightened intuition told me something was amiss at my office. I felt an instinct to lay low and keep my head down, kind of a natural response to the fact that I felt someone was trying to kill me.

I realized in 2018, that the idea of Farbod ever paying my commission on Hualapai and Farm was ridiculous. He would get super upset over meager sums. He would nitpick me over $100 or $200—screaming for, it would seem, two hours at night over some small amount of money for months on end. It was absurd to think he would pay a commission the size Hualapai and Farm would generate.

A final note about Farbod's business partner, Ray Ghouli, that demonstrates he hung around a nefarious crowd.

A couple of years after this first encounter at the Oasis RV Park, in 2018, Farbod and I were driving to West Henderson to look at a two-and-one-half acre parcel of land.

Farbod was telling me how much Ray Ghouli complained about me. This was something I heard on a regular basis after my car wreck. It had not happened at all before, but now, Ray Ghouli was complaining about me behind my back—for no good reason, of course. I thought of myself as one of the hardest-working brokers out there, and I invested in marketing my listings, unlike many others.

But that day, on that car ride to West Henderson, Farbod Sattari confided in me that Ghouli did not have any money of his own. I asked Farbod to tell me more. I assumed Ray Ghouli had 100 percent ownership of the Oasis RV Park, but Farbod said Ray Ghouli had a "money guy" who was the real buyer on most of Ghouli's properties. He would give Ghouli 10 percent ownership to manage the property for him. Ray, who was always going around acting like he had more money than everyone, was really just a glorified property manager.

A former client told me that Ray Ghouli would buy properties through none other than Ezri Namvar—the infamous "Bernie Madoff of Beverly Hills."

By 2018, the name Ezri Namvar was as well-known on the West Coast as the notorious name Bernie Madoff was known all over the world. In the wake of the financial crisis in 2007 and 2008, the bankruptcy of Namvar's Namco Capital Group led to $1 billion in claims from investors. Authorities said Namvar's business constituted a classic Ponzi scheme, with new investors paying off old. In 2011, Namvar was sentenced to seven years in prison.

Namvar had been a longtime leading businessman and philanthropist. Many of his clients were members of the tight-knit Iranian-Jewish community of Beverly Hills. One newspaper (*LA Weekly*) called him a "gangster." I didn't have to look far into the backgrounds of those around me to see trouble.

There was darkness everywhere.

There were also strange things that the Sattaris did that they probably thought would help me get over how poorly things had gone with Hualapai and Farm. Rumors were swirling around town that Farbod was in escrow with Richmond American on the land. *How could that be possible?* I had an exclusive listing on the property at the time, and I was procuring cause with Richmond American. (Procuring cause is a process to determine if a broker has earned a commission on a property.)

Mordred started saying prison felons were looking for me and assaulting him. Before he left my office, he disappeared for over a week, claiming he'd been assaulted because he worked for me. Mordred claimed he was attacked at a place called Stoney's. After he left, Mordred, Farbod, and Nahid were claiming prison felons were harassing them, looking for me. I felt they were giving me powerful clues. I just could not put my finger on it. What did all these people know about my wreck that I did not know? It was as if I were close to the endgame. I felt the presence of Elohim with me the whole time, somehow protecting me.

Farbod said he was followed leaving Queensridge, and he was slapped around at Wahoo Tacos at Boca Park by someone who wanted to know where I lived.

Nahid mentioned she was at a Target parking lot loading groceries, when a guy came up to assist her. She said that as he helped her load her groceries, he started asking about me.

Mordred claimed he was being harassed at a bar at Flamingo and I-215 next to my office, claiming people were looking for me. He called me when the supposed altercation was taking place, screaming hysterically into the phone. I was thinking to myself, *this guy has walked right out of a comic book. He has left my brokerage and now all this drama, still about me.*

Farbod gave me the listing again at Hualapai and Farm as a distraction when he went into escrow with Mike Levin behind my back in 2017. And now rumors were swirling that Farbod was in escrow with Richmond American? I had breakfast with the decision-maker on this land with both Richmond and Farbod. I did not want to believe the rumors.

Around this time, Mordred was incessantly nagging me to let him serve as my broker on property owned by my pension plan. It was a two-acre parcel near Decatur and Shelbourne. Mordred wanted to be my broker and list the property. When an agent becomes your broker, he owes you loyalty and honesty and fair dealings, along with many other fiduciary duties. I had a powerful feeling from the universe, from Elohim, that I should hire him. I saw it as an opportunity for someone who had not treated me honestly in the past to do so now. Should I trust Mordred? I knew the listing felt right in every fiber of my being. If he were to threaten me or if he treated me dishonestly, then he would be delivered into my hands by God. I also knew I would still have to maintain a relationship with Mordred because of the tens of millions of dollars in listings I had with his father.

Mordred showed up at my office one morning after my litigation was filed like the silent specter of death. Mordred referred me to a buyer to purchase his father's seventeen acres of land at Patrick and I-215.

Mordred told me that his father had qualified the buyer and that he knew the lead was legitimate. But when he gave me the lead, he could not look me in the eye. Mordred also said that his family loved me so much that his father was giving me an entire 6 percent of a $20 million deal. Farbod, who would scream at me for months over $100, now wants to hand me $1.2 million? I felt it was to distract me from what was going on with Hualapai and Farm. What was this all about? A tingling sensation went through me. Was this the assassination Elohim had spoken to me about when I left the car wreck demanding more proof that this was attempted murder? My senses told me this was the moment I had been waiting for. It was a powerful thought that I couldn't shake. I was on guard.

. . . .

I questioned Farbod and Mordred about this referral dozens of times. Farbod and Mordred both told me how legitimate the buyer was, and that they had both checked him out. I asked again about Hualapai and Farm being in escrow with Richmond, and Farbod said not to listen to false rumors around town, that I was loved so much in their family that they were giving me the buyer for Patrick and I-215. Farbod reiterated they were going to pay me 6 percent of the sales price—over a million dollars of a $20 million sale. In fact, $1.2 million to be precise. It could be a tremendous paycheck—big enough for some people to retire.

Shortly after I was given this lead, that was when Mordred called me up and asked if I parked both of my cars in the garage. I felt God was giving me another powerful clue. Did Mordred have me tracked before the failed murder attempt on my life?

"I can't fit both of my cars in my garage," he said. "Is yours big enough?" he asked.

When I was given the buyer lead on Patrick and 215, Mike Gonzales left my office like a thief in the night. He called me up and asked me to come to the office. When I arrived that Monday morning in March 2018, all his stuff was gone. He asked me to sign a form to relocate his license. I signed the form at his request. At least Mike did not steal his license off my wall like Mordred did. Gonzales told me he was going to work for

Elite Realty and wanted a change. I didn't mind seeing him go. In my mind, it was *good riddance.*

The potential buyer for Patrick and I-215 texted all the time about meeting with me. The prospect never gave me his name. His excuse was that he did not want to be in a commission dispute, so he wanted to remain anonymous until the transaction went through. He used a cell phone number from Miami, and then a couple of weeks later, one from Marathon, Florida. The cell phones were burner phones. *Ridiculous.* Why would someone purchasing a $20 million parcel of land use burner cell phones?

Then, to bolster the buyer's credibility, the buyer invited me and Mordred to a Golden Knights hockey game with front-row seats. I should say, *alleged* credibility. I declined this meeting. It did not feel right. Why would I meet with someone who refuses to give me their name?

Mordred told me he met with the buyer at the hockey game. He claimed he had a great time, that they had seats worth several thousand dollars each. He said he met with both the buyer and his girlfriend.

After the Golden Knights game that Mordred claimed he attended with this anonymous buyer, the buyer texted me the next day. He wanted to meet me at the land. At 9:30 at night.

"Why do you want to meet anyone at 9:30 at night?" I texted back.

He replied that his partner did not want to go alone, and she was female. She wanted, the buyer said, to get pictures of the strip from drones from the site late at night. The anonymous buyer said he would ask Mordred to handle the meeting if I did not want to do it.

"You do that," I replied in a text.

I have never met with people on vacant parcels of land late at night. I did not like to meet buyers at vacant parcels—*period.* If a possible buyer could not make up his mind if he wanted to buy the parcel without walking the property with me, it threw off bells and whistles.

At the time, I was reading Book 6 of Stephen King's "Dark Tower" series—*Song of Susannah.* In the story, Father Callahan was lured to his death by a bunch of vampires pretending to be a legitimate business that wanted to donate a million dollars to Father Callahan's charity. They were looking to murder him, and not just in this universe, but the entire multiverse of existence! Somehow, I felt the story was mirroring my own. I took it as a profound sign from my lord Elohim.

I immediately texted Mordred and Farbod that night and told them I thought this buyer was bullshit and that something more insidious was at work.

Farbod and Mordred both called me. I told Farbod my concerns, and he agreed that we should call off the meeting with the buyer. Mordred, on the other hand, was insistent that I was wrong. I noticed Mordred sounded nervous.

I told him my concerns, that I believed the person who had been behind the text messages was Mike Levin.

By now, my car wreck case was filed in the federal courts—car wrecks are very rarely in the federal courts. I saw the connection to Mike Levin immediately with my enhanced intuition, my PTSD.

The fear coming out of Mordred was like the fear that came out of his father.

The next day, Mordred called me at 6:00 a.m. He was scared, and he tried to convince me that the buyer for the land was legitimate. He told me that if I didn't hammer out a deal with the buyer, then he would end up buying from a couple of other competing land brokers. I could hear his voice quivering. Why would Mordred be concerned that I had figured out Mike Levin was the fake buyer on Patrick and I-215?

There will be more murder attempts on your life when you enter litigation and those responsible will be revealed. This was what God wanted to reveal to me when I drove from the scene of my murder.

Mordred called my office again that morning at 7:30. He was still my broker on Decatur and Shelbourne, and that property had gone into escrow with a buyer he had found by himself.

He wanted to charge me a transaction fee. I had already agreed to pay him 4 percent if he found the buyer himself, which would mean he was getting both ends of the deal as the seller's agent and buyer's agent. I told him that commissions and transaction fees were already spelled out in the contract. I also repeated my concerns regarding Mike Levin.

He went into a fury and threatened my life as well as my new assistant, Jody Szakara. I was stunned and shaken from the experience. Farbod immediately called, and I told him what happened. He had Mordred call and apologize to me. He was supposed to apologize to Jody also, but he never did.

The next day, I took Jessamine to lunch.

Usually, I would take Jessamine and Jody to lunch, but this day, Jody decided not to go. During our lunch, Jessamine told me that I needed to be careful of her brother.

Suddenly, I was very worried. This was no game. This was real. Everything I had feared about this whole situation was dropping into place.

Jessamine did not pull any punches. She said Mordred had wanted me dead on three separate occasions. She said Mordred had the means and know-how to get it done. She said Mordred also knew the people who could carry it out and had the expertise.

I saw this as a perfect description of the driver who hit me. The driver who hit me knew what he was doing. The driver who tried to get me to commit insurance fraud by saying I was moving and, when I did not agree, went into a violent rage. The same driver that did not want us to go through discovery, finding out certain things about his past. It was powerful.

I was stunned.

I showed Mordred's sister the bridge—explaining my theory about Mike Levin. I started going over all the coincidences. She was startled. I showed her many circumstantial pieces of evidence that tied him to my murder. In the federal courts, discovery is really short. Mike Levin knows the federal process, since he is a former FBI agent. Mike would want me dead before I went into discovery to protect the assassin.

I told her Mordred tried to murder me through Mike Levin.

"No," she said. "Mike, no—I did not mean it."

Too late.

It's hard to take back a confession of attempted murder. I realized immediately that Jessamine had lifted the fog of the car wreck.

The next day, Jessamine came to my office.

Ironically, on the same day, I had a full-price offer to deliver to her father on Hualapai and Farm. The offer was from KB Home. After all these years of work, I had a full-price offer. Not only did I have a full-price offer, but the deal would close in just thirty days! That was unheard of since the financial crisis. When it came to a national home builder, they needed all their zoning in place before they would close. They got all their money from Wall Street and were not allowed to speculate on land. If they bought land, they were creating subdivisions. I told Jessamine that if she was able to get her father to accept the offer, I would give her half the commission, which would come to $240,000.

I knew after the previous day's lunch meeting with Jessamine, that everything was revealed. I knew that my car wreck, beyond a doubt, was tied to Hualapai and Farm. There were too many rumors about it being in escrow with Richmond American. I had to find out the truth. Farbod now had his 30-day deal he had always wanted.

She went crazy—the wrong way. I thought she would be thrilled at the proposal, but she started yelling that this was sexual harassment. How was that possible? She confessed that her brother was dangerous and wanted me dead on three separate occasions, pretty much confessing three murder attempts on my life the day before, and now she was claiming sexual harassment? This made no sense.

I soon realized that it did make sense; she was creating a fake fire to distract from the main issue: her confession about Mordred and the three times he tried to murder me.

I stewed over everything that weekend.

My PTSD went off, big time. I knew to trust it. It dawned on me that perhaps the Hualapai and Farm file had been stolen from my office.

Sure enough, when I went in to work on Monday morning, the file was gone. Jody and I went through all the files in the office, and then we went through all the files in storage. No luck.

I went into a rage. I ripped Jessamine and Nahid's real estate licenses from my wall, and I marched them straight down to the real estate division to turn them in.

Mordred called me to try and calm things down. I told him about my listing on Hualapai and Farm, and that I was procuring cause with Richmond, and I needed to get paid on the sale. I also told him about the offer from KB Home closing in thirty days!

"Are you sure you've got a copy of the listing at your office?" he taunted.

I bluffed. I told him I made a copy of it; yes.

"*Eww*," said Mordred. "That was smart."

Later that day, I got an email from Nahid claiming I did not put a termination date in the listing. In my opinion, it was an admission they stole the listing from my office.

My intuition was going off bells and whistles, telling me Mordred took the listing from his father while working at my firm, and he was the one who was supposed to date it. I realized it might have been done like that intentionally to sabotage my business if I ever pieced together the car wreck.

Farbod started taunting me that someone dug a hole on a property he owned at Warm Springs and Durango that resembled a grave that he thought was there for me. Why would he mention a grave? At first, he said, it must be his rival Kay Roohani. Then he said maybe a guy named Roger Crow. Then, the last person he blamed was former Governor Sisolak. According to Farbod, he had loaned former Governor Sisolak around $10 million, many years prior, to start up his 99-cent store.

When I was trying to sell the KB Home property at Windmill and Lindell, I was a little on the aggressive side with Sisolak, trying to get the right zoning approved. It was a little comical that Farbod Sattari was saying my own governor might have been behind this. Former Governor Sisolak was not governor yet, but he was very close to becoming governor when this went down.

Farbod started taunting me about how he was being slapped around by felons who wanted to know where I live. Farbod then mentioned how his son and his wife were being harassed by people wanting to know where I was. Farbod insisted the hole was dug for me. And I said something that shocked Farbod Sattari down to his core.

"It is none of these people who you are naming," I said.

"Who is it then?" he said.

"It has to be Mike Levin," I responded.

The silence that followed was the deepest silence I have ever heard. That's when the Sattaris started getting afraid.

Very, very, very afraid.

Farbod's voice started trembling. It was unnerving, as I had never heard Farbod scared before.

"Mike, whatever you want to do, Nahid and I are one hundred percent behind you," he said.

The next night I get a call from Farbod saying that Mike Levin had never heard of me and you have never heard of him in your federal court case. Farbod told me that Jessamine saw everything I told her as the truth.

I was in shock. Why would Farbod Sattari call me to tell me that?

It was around this same time Farbod started calling me nightly to say that I must learn to fear Mordred. When the car wreck first happened, he would call saying Mordred would never cause me bodily harm, and now he was saying the opposite.

Saying the name "Mike Levin" out loud was almost a kind of code. I didn't have to say anything else.

Once I mentioned Mike Levin was behind the text messages, no member of the Sattari family mentioned again that people were harassing them while looking for me. Nahid tried to claim she was just joking about being harassed. The Sattari family was scared. I never received a text message ever again regarding the buyer Mordred and Farbod referred to me after I mentioned it was Mike Levin. Mordred never again said he was being assaulted by people who were looking for me. At this time, I emailed Farbod and his wife about my near-death experience. I told them about the message from God. Farbod said he never wanted to hear about this ever again.

That's when I fired Farbod Sattari as my client, and I returned the tens of millions in listed properties. They could find another broker to sell them. I didn't want to work for a client who thought he had the right to pick away at my life. I realized the listings were an illusion and a false security blanket. Once I realized the Hualapai and Farm listing was missing, I took Nahid's and Jessamine's licenses off my wall and turned the licenses in to the state real estate division. I drove straight down there and did not look back. When Farbod found this out, he threatened to sue me for terminating his family from my office. But it was my office, and if someone was making me uncomfortable in my own business, then they were gone.

Next, I gave notice to Farbod that I would be relocating my real estate company. This was one family that I no longer wanted to be part of—ever.

I was not going to be lured to my death by my own greed. I realized that Farbod, by making false promises about being his lifetime broker, had strung me along. His son felt as if he had a right to pick away at my life. I was no longer part of the Sattaris. I became deeply saddened thinking of my violent car wreck and dying for people so rich.

I reached out to Richmond before they closed Hualapai and Farm right after I fired Farbod, and Richmond paid me a $80,000 commission, knowing that I earned the fee and put the deal together. Farbod told me years before that God does not let you get burned on deals because of how generous you are. His words proved correct it seemed.

CHAPTER 23

My Sworn Testimony

The offer came one week after the depositions were complete. Obviously, they did not want to go to trial. The lawyers knew my integrity, and the details were all on my side.

So was my credibility, under oath. Depositions, after all, are sworn testimony. The settlement offer speaks for itself.

One million dollars.

If you watch my deposition and truck driver Benjamin Troy Mangum's deposition, you will hear two very different accounts of what happened when Mangum rear-ended me.

When I was murdered and came back.

At first, the lawyers defending Mangum tried to dig into some of my past. They were curious about my broken, unhinged jaw from jiu-jitsu in April 2013, and they wanted to know why it took me eighteen months to visit a doctor after that injury.

"I was hoping the stinging would go away, and it never did," I testified. This showed a history of me not going to the doctor when I became seriously hurt.

The fact I had resisted seeking medical help certainly showed that I wasn't one to immediately seek care after being harmed—and it also fit the pattern with how long I waited after the car wreck. I think this fact was a huge point in my favor. If I thought the rear-end collision was a chance to score some quick money, I would have called an ambulance-chasing attorney very quickly. But I waited weeks to even acknowledge what had really happened to me, let alone to go see doctors and figure out why I was feeling the way I did. All I wanted to do, as I have mentioned many times, is move on with my life.

In January 2012, I also had my elbow hyper-extended during martial arts training. The lawyers were clearly trying to insinuate that my car wreck injuries were possibly the result of jiu-jitsu or kenpo karate, although they didn't come out and say it in such a straightforward fashion. I knew when it came to litigation, if you did not tell the truth and tell them your complete history, it would be used against you, and you would be made to look like a liar. I was brutally honest in my deposition and in disclosing all my medical history, including the fact that I had a medical recommendation for marijuana.

They were looking for all sorts of potential things I might have to explain in front of a jury that they could try to use against me. But there was nothing. In my deposition, I was credible when it came to all of their points. I didn't ask for or receive a State of Nevada medical marijuana card until after the car wreck. It was when I was wasting away to nothing that I finally went out and sought a state medical marijuana card. I was desperate to gain my weight back and figured the munchies would probably help.

The lawyers wanted to know about an injury I had in the U.S. Navy and an injury with a cargo door while I was working at Southwest Airlines. Perhaps they were trying to show a pattern of my injuries; I'll never know for sure. The Navy injury hurt my lower back, and the Southwest Airlines injury hurt my neck. Both injuries were very old.

The attorney tried to press me on the naval accident, insinuating that I got some medical discharge or general conduct discharge from the military. He was grasping for whatever straw he could find. I told him I received an honorable discharge, and I was a two-time nationally decorated Gulf War veteran.

I was offended that the attorney was attacking my military service. I fought hard for this country. Maybe I did not see actual combat, but I served during a war. I was honorably discharged.

But, again, they offered that $1 million.

The fact that I could testify that I had lost a large amount of weight after the car wreck was further evidence that I'd been through something traumatic. I had the foresight to make a copy of my old driver's license and my new driver's license. The old license photo had been taken three months before my wreck. The new one was taken three months after. The contrast revealed a profound change in my physical appearance. The after picture showed my very gaunt face. You could see the trauma I went through merely by looking into my eyes.

They tried to press me on details for what happened immediately after the wreck—whether I had continued to my lawyer's office to discuss the IRS audit into a 401(k) account that I managed.

They showed me a photo of the Lexus I was driving. The photo was taken after the accident and before any repairs were completed, but it didn't show any of the compaction damage inside the trunk. You could not see the damage unless you opened the trunk. Yes, the Lexus was operable. They wanted to know if I used that car to drive to meet my lawyers after the wreck. I told the lawyers I didn't remember much of anything, but I did remember driving to see my lawyers and then running other errands later that day. In fact, as you know by now, the entire month or month and a half after the wreck was a blur. Very few details.

They wanted to know what I had done prior to the wreck, including what time I had gotten out of bed and what I had for breakfast. Of course, I told them I couldn't remember what time I had woken up, but I had not eaten breakfast—I had been on my way to Del Taco for a breakfast burrito when the wreck happened.

They asked me about what medications I was taking prior to the accident, and I told them I couldn't recall.

Then they came back to more photos of my car.

Had I looked at the truck to check his vehicle for damage?

Yes, the accident did push in the front bumper. It was a crease in the bumper. It also caused compaction damage.

Had I already been to Del Taco when it happened?

No.

Your vehicle was traveling in which direction?

I wasn't traveling. I was fully stopped. (This was a trick question.)

Which way were you going to turn?

Left. That's why I was looking left.

You were at a stop at the stop sign?

Yes.

You were depressing the brake?

(Another trick question! Depressing—is that the opposite of "pressing" the brake? I didn't fall for it.) If you think about it, you can construe it both ways, so I clarified for them when I spoke.

Yes. Fully braked.

That vehicle has power brakes?

I don't know. Check with Lexus.

How long were you stopped before the accident happened?

Maybe a second or two.

Did you ever see the truck before it struck the back of your car?

No.

What did you hear?

I didn't hear anything. I didn't hear any braking or anything. All of a sudden, I was looking left, and my head got snapped around like I was in a rodeo, and then I lost consciousness . . . felt like my brain was ricocheting in my skull.

I knew with my case in the federal courts I could not tell them about my experience in the afterlife or what God told me. This was not the time or place to talk of my death. I left it that I was unconscious. That part weighed on my soul as I had taken an oath of God when I took my deposition.

Later in mediation, out of guilt for not talking about the afterlife, I did tell the judge how I actually died, minus the message from Elohim. I could tell he believed me. He was also horrified by the contrasting driver's license photos.

Back in the deposition, the lawyer asked, "Did your head strike anything inside the vehicle?"

I don't know.

It was funny they asked me this question, as this was all I'd thought about since I died: what did my head hit, if it hit anything? Did it hit the headrest? That seems very likely given the intensity of the rear-end collision.

Did you have any visible signs of injury? Something you could see?

No. I looked everywhere after I was hit and did not see any blood anywhere.

How long were you being thrown around like you were in a rodeo?

It's a guess—I'd say a few seconds.

Which way was your head thrown first?

I don't know.

The lawyers wanted to know if the police were called or if a police report was ever filled out. No and no.

I explained that the driver of the truck wanted to call an ambulance. I told them I wanted to shake off the moment and move on with my life. I told them we moved the vehicles in front of the Del Taco to exchange information and that the driver asked me to do him a favor—he wanted me to tell my insurance company that I was moving at the time of the wreck. I said that I told the driver *no way* and that I was fully braked, and then the driver got confrontational with me, so I got the hell out of there.

I told them it felt as if it was intentional. It was as if this driver knew which kind of wrecks were deadly.

When you sought medical care, did you tell them that you had lost consciousness?

I don't remember.

The lawyer asked me whether I had climbed out of the car at the four-way stop, and I told them yes, I had. I told them we moved to the parking spaces by the Del Taco, had a conversation, and exchanged insurance information.

I was asked to describe the driver, and I couldn't really say. I was asked what I was wearing that day, and I said I did not remember. I told them that one thing I remembered was the confrontation because it left an imprint on my memory.

Did the driver of the truck appear to be injured?

No.

Can you estimate how long you were standing outside the vehicles talking with this Wadman employee?

About five minutes.

What did you recall, sir, about how you were feeling from that evening when you reported the accident to your insurance company and when you presented at the Phillips clinic six weeks later?

I had a feeling of being shaken up and a feeling of shock, like the crash just happened a second ago. It's true to this day—I feel that shock wave from the crash going through me.

But you didn't seek care for six weeks?

Yes.

Were you concerned?

Yes.

You had a family physician at the clinic?

Yes.

You could have called him at any time in those six weeks?

Yes.

And you kept working?

Yes—at a diminished level.

Did you complain of this shock feeling when you presented to the Phillips clinic?

I don't remember.

What did Dr. Phillips tell you was wrong with you?

I don't remember.

I noticed he brought up Dr. Phillips a lot—a doctor I fired for treating me inappropriately. Dr. Phillips was still haunting me and stalking me, even after I fired him for inappropriate behavior.

When did you hire a lawyer?

April of 2016.

They really wanted me to say how I had been referred to Nevada Brain and Spine Care, to Dr. Nagy. They pressed, but I couldn't remember or say who had referred me. For obvious reasons, they suggested it might be my lawyer. They wanted to paint a picture of my attorney creating this case for me.

Again, the lawyer for Wadman circled back around to ask how long after the car wreck I had gotten my medical marijuana card, and which doctor had given me the card. They wanted to know who suggested I go get a medical marijuana card—and it happened to be my good, longtime friend and osteopath, Dr. Randy Birdman. He saw me at his house and examined me at the end of March 2016. He saw how wasted away I was. Dr. Birdman was always a very skinny person, and when I saw him, I was skinnier than he was.

Dr. Birdman, I told the lawyer, immediately said I had a traumatic brain injury. He gave me advice about three or four different times. They wanted me to explain all the doctors who had looked at me, including a doctor who had done a nerve study.

The lawyer wanted to know when I gained the weight back, and I told him that it was about a month or so after getting my medical marijuana card. The marijuana gave me the munchies.

It was funny that they were trying to make my injury about cannabis use rather than what was done to me. This was 2019. It was a different ball game with the widespread legalization of marijuana. Times were changing, and this was one of the worst defenses for anyone who hurts others. He obviously had Theresa Stempien's report.

The lawyer had me run through all of my treatments and all of the various doctors and therapists who provided me those treatments. The bottom line was that my injuries were severe. I detailed the list of medications I was taking as well—for depression, pain, everything. I also detailed how it impacted my day-to-day life, particularly my mental processing. In retrospect, I believe this was one of the more powerful moments in the deposition.

For instance, I told them I would go to pay bills, and as soon as I left my surroundings to do that task, I would forget what I intended to do unless I vocalized my thoughts out loud.

Here's a direct quote of mine from the deposition:

"I still feel the shock wave like it happened a second ago. I have a pressure that is always on the right side of my skull that a lot of the time turns into a pressure headache. I have back pain now, neck pain. I know it (the scans) shows protrusions in my mid-back, but I don't feel that as much as my low-back and my neck. I was never depressed before, and it created a depression in my life. I have a harder time multi-tasking. I'm having to come home during the day—I'm very blessed that I'm able to—to take naps because when I go to sleep at night, I'm only sleeping like an hour or two at night, and it's only a very light, twilight sleep. So I have to take naps during the day a lot."

I told them the pressure in my head is always there, knowing that the wreck is always in the back of my mind. "I wouldn't be here right now if it was just my spine," I said. "It was a very, very, very hard wreck for anyone to live with. You can't put a price on it. I wouldn't take this injury for a trillion dollars . . . I have a feeling of shock like it happened a second ago."

I told the lawyer that I had lost considerable amounts of money since the wreck. Not only had I experienced a serious drop in income, but in 2016, 2017, and 2018, the Las Vegas real estate market was a lot hotter than before the car wreck; I should have been making more money than in the years prior.

And, finally, I told them about my "filter damage" and its impact on all relationships—romantic, family, and all over the board.

Anybody watching the video deposition would know I was a credible witness who had been severely hurt. Anybody watching the video deposition would know I had a clear story of the events and the resulting damage done to my brain and body.

In fact, the lawyer knew it too. Why else would they have offered the money to *not* take it to trial?

The lawyer wanted to know what else I would tell a jury. I told him I would talk about pressure and time. "It was pressure and time that created the Grand Canyon, it was pressure and time that allowed Andy Dufresne to escape from Shawshank prison, and it was pressure and time that were eroding my right hippocampus." I told him all of this.

I could tell the attorney for the driver did not like my answer; he did not have any more questions.

CHAPTER 24

Strange "Facts" Under Oath

I was good—clear, certain, and factual.

But Benjamin Troy Mangum, in his deposition, made a ton of strategic mistakes. The biggest one of all was right at the end, when he officially lost it and got angry. You could see him bristle and lose control of his emotions. He revealed his true colors at the end—and his lawyers knew he wouldn't be a good witness to put in front of a jury.

Let me count the number of ways.

First, however, some background.

Mangum said he had worked with Wadman Corporation for thirty-one years, nearly half of the construction firm's existence. Wadman, based in Utah, builds new commercial construction all over the country. Pharmacies, Walgreens, grocery stores, and even a few Mormon temples and churches. The company is affiliated with the Church of Jesus Christ of Latter-day Saints. (When this was revealed to me later, I became deeply offended. The Mormons had sent elders to my house to give me blessings right after I was hurt. I felt Mangum was trying to hide behind the Mormon church. By the way, when the elders of the Mormon church came over to give me blessings to heal, this was when the sacred name of God was revealed to me to be Elohim.)

Mangum had started out with Wadman as a concrete finisher, then became a wood framer and finish carpenter before moving up the ranks to superintendent in 1987.

At the time of the wreck, Mangum was overseeing the construction of the American First Credit Union project in Summerlin, the master-planned community in Las Vegas. Mangum had started on the project two months before the car wreck in the parking lot. While he lived in St. George, Utah, Mangum would spend the week in Las Vegas, where he was overseeing projects, and then drive home for the weekend—in his company truck.

Mangum admitted to a couple of previous traffic violations, including getting a speeding ticket in St. George for driving five miles over the speed limit on a two-lane highway. He said he had received "less than five" traffic violations over the previous twenty years.

However, there was also a motor vehicle collision he was involved in, back in 2007, when he claimed to have been in a four-car chain reaction. This accident played an eerie coincidence in the evidence around my car wreck. What happened, according to Mangum, is that he was the one who got rear-ended. He was driving for Wadman Corporation at the time.

Mangum said he was stopped at a stop light and got hit so hard that he rear-ended the car in front of him and *that* vehicle rear-ended the next car too. Mangum said he was the one who was cited because the driver of the car that hit him—the one that started the entire accident—fled the scene and was never identified.

How convenient for Benjamin Mangum.

"The guy that hit me took off, and nobody got his license number, so I was the one at fault," Mangum claimed. Asked if he felt at fault for the 2007 accident, Mangum said, "No."

At the time, Mangum was driving a three-quarter-ton pickup, a Chevy Silverado, just like the one he rammed into my car. The only difference is that he rear-ended me with a full-one-ton pickup. What are the odds that he gets in a similar accident nine years later with the same type of vehicle?

It threw a chill down my spine when I saw this part of his deposition. Did the person he rear-ended in 2007 become seriously injured? Or did that person die? And how many wrecks in Chevy trucks can someone get into before law enforcement looks at this as suspicious?

Mangum said he was familiar with the shopping center where my car wreck happened in 2016. He was driving east on Charleston and made a left into the Albertsons shopping center. Mangum said he wanted to drop a package off at a FedEx location. Another coincidence: I was driving east on Charleston when I turned into the parking lot to go to Del Taco. However, he said he was *looking for a* FedEx. While he was familiar with the shopping center and had been to Albertsons, he said he entered the parking lot believing he would find a FedEx drop-off location.

However, there were some strange facts in his version of events. First, he claimed that we didn't get out of our cars when he first hit me. "When I bumped him, we both pulled left and right into that parking stall," he said.

"Right after the contact, you never got out of your vehicle?" asked my lawyer.

"No, not at all," said Mangum.

This is pure baloney.

I knew better than to move the vehicles after a motor vehicle collision. When I came back to my body, after having died and returned, I immediately opened my door and went to see what had transpired. Mangum was standing outside my car. After a minute or two, we decided to move both cars around to the parking lot. That was when Mangum assessed the damage to my car. And that was when he asked me to do him a "favor" and say that I was moving when I reported it to my insurance company—to say that I wasn't fully stopped when he plowed into me.

Mangum testified in the deposition that the wreck caused a crease in the front bumper around the license plate of his pickup, and that he did the repairs himself. He said he was the only project superintendent who worked on his company truck and that he kept a shop at his home to do such work. He claimed that Wadman paid for the damaged part, which Mangum purchased at a Chevy dealership for $360. Mangum said the damage on his truck included a "crease" in the "middle part" of the three-part bumper, and that's what he replaced.

Before working for Wadman, Mangum had worked in maintenance as a "service writer" at a Chevy dealership. He gave customers estimates of how much various services would cost. As a result, he knew how to take care of such damage by himself. Unfortunately, he didn't think through how this might look later; if he had taken the truck to an auto repair specialist, it would have created a more official record of the damage and the cost for the repairs. They would have read the black box, which I believe would have shown him speed up right before the collision. I know his lawyer was thinking that a potential jury would scratch their heads and say, "That's fishy."

My lawyer pressed Mangum on why he decided to get down on his back and feel around under my car.

Mangum *claimed* there was no damage to my car. "We both investigated his car pretty thoroughly," he said, overlooking the fact that my insurance company paid $4,000 to cover the cost of repairs to my Lexus.

Mangum tried to say we both lay on the ground together, looking underneath the bumper. This did not happen at all. I wouldn't lie on the ground with someone after God told me they tried to murder me. I believe he said I was lying on the ground as a feeble attempt to show that I was not hurt. He tried to say I just drove off after he rear-ended me. That couldn't be further from the truth. The guy had literally sent me to my Maker.

My lawyer to Mangum: "Why did you feel it necessary to lie on the ground and feel it?"

Mangum: "I wanted to make sure Mr. Longi's car was fine."

My lawyer: "Was there any discussion about calling the police?"

Mangum: "Police don't come to private parking lots."

(Note: it's funny how Mangum knew this fact so well. It was as if he knew all the laws when it came to motor vehicle collisions.)

My attorney deposed Mangum the way a police officer deposes a criminal.

"Did you ask Mr. Longi to lie to the insurance?"

Mangum said he did not. (A lie.)

"Did you ask Mr. Longi to say his car was moving at the time of impact?"

Mangum said he did not. (A lie.)

"Did you try to intimidate Mr. Longi?"

"No." (A lie.)

"Did Mr. Longi appear to be intimidated by you?"

"No." (A lie.)

I know Mangum was lying because after he tried to get me to commit insurance fraud, I got the hell out of there. I bolted so quickly I did not even get Mangum's driver's license, although I did have his insurance information and a few photos. I knew this guy to be a total creeper.

My lawyer: "Was there some discussion about contacting medical?"

Mangum: "When he got out of his vehicle, he was kind of holding his neck, like he was really hurt."

In the video, at this point, Mangum reaches up with his right arm and grabs the left side of his neck. This was true. Except it took place at the spot where the wreck happened, not in front of the Del Taco, where we moved after the initial conversation. It threw another chill down my spine. Now I know why I was being taunted about my neck by Travis Nelson. How many people did this creep brag to about what he did to me? Nevada Title got the pig farm and Hualapai and Farm deal. Too many disturbing coincidences.

More Mangum: "When I got out of the vehicle and seen him doing that, I asked him if he was okay. He said, 'I don't know at the moment.' I said, do you need medical assistance? He didn't reply. I asked him a second time, he didn't reply. A third time, he replied, 'No, I'm fine, I'm a little sore in the neck.'"

In my recollection anyway, he asked many more times than that.

Mangum didn't know I had just died. I was woozy and disoriented—my head had been snapped around like I was riding in a rodeo, but a lot worse. My head felt like it had been shaken by the hand of God.

Asked to go through the wreck blow by blow, Mangum made a huge mistake that blew any chance he would be perceived as credible by a future potential jury.

He claimed that he had kept a car length's distance between himself and the back of my car as we approached the four-way stop.

Really? Why would you do that? Once you turn into the shopping center, the road runs between McDonald's to the right and Del Taco to the left before coming to the four-way stop. There is probably room for about eight to ten vehicles on that road before the four-way stop (without backing up onto Charleston). Why would you ever leave a *full* car length of space between yourself and the car in front of you? Nobody does that. A few feet? Sure. A full car length? That wasn't a realistic claim on his part.

But here's the issue. Mangum, in the deposition, asserts vehemently that he was going two miles per hour at most when he hit me. He also claimed that I stopped at the four-way stop, pulled out, and stopped suddenly again. He claimed, basically, that I double-stopped. He insinuated that the collision was my fault.

But there's a big problem with that line of thinking. If he had kept a full car length of space between himself and the back of my vehicle, my alleged double-stop would not have mattered! He should have had plenty of time to note that he also needed to stop again. Of course, I did no such double-stop. And no juror is going to buy the one car length of open space *because he rear-ended me!* And nobody is going to buy the two miles-per-hour business *because my car was damaged to the tune of over $4,000, and I received a traumatic brain injury and injuries to my spine.*

In addition, Mangum claimed he was looking "straight forward" the entire time. Again, if he was a full car length's distance behind me, his eyes were looking "straight forward," and he was only going two miles an hour, he would have had plenty of time to stop, to avoid smacking me. Asked if he was "distracted at all," Mangum insisted he was not.

Clearly, by definition, he *was* distracted. A driver who was paying attention would have avoided the wreck. Either that or there was intent.

Mangum claimed that since his airbags didn't deploy, he couldn't have been going very fast—he said the bags had deployed in the accident back in 2007, and that was, he claimed, a much more serious rear-end crunch. In fact, the insurance company totaled the pickup he was driving in that 2007 crash.

He said his knowledge as a service writer for the Chevy dealership gave him special insight into the speeds needed to trigger airbags—and he even denied analysis from his team's own experts that he was likely going up to five miles per hour. How strange his previous job before working for Wadman was at Chevrolet, and he gets into multiple mid-rear collisions in Chevrolet Silverado pickup trucks.

Mangum conveniently overlooked the fact that he was driving a one-ton dually pickup with a loaded toolbox. A one-ton pickup weighs close to 10,000 pounds. If he was rolling over that open gap between us—a full car length—he was certainly going over two miles per hour! And if he wasn't watching the road in front of him, what was he watching? What was he looking at? If he wanted to keep a full car length between us, why didn't he? Why did he let that gap close?

Conveniently, Mangum claimed there was a witness to the wreck. He claimed he got the license plate of the witness (but not the person's name or address), and he claimed this witness came forward only after I had left the scene. But the slip of paper he used to jot down the license plate number was accidentally left behind the visor of the 2001 Chevy pickup when he turned it in to Wadman for a new vehicle in 2017.

How convenient for Benjamin Troy Mangum—he gets rid of the truck right before my lawsuit. He obviously knew it was coming.

Mangum was also hard to pin down about whether he had seen my brake lights go on. Asked if he could have done anything differently at all to avoid the accident, Mangum seemed confused by the question. He finally said there was nothing he could have done differently. And when asked about the vehicle's black box, the computer that stores information that's useful in analyzing collisions, Mangum said he was under the assumption that the data should have been retained. But it wasn't. It was stripped clean. Again, very convenient and very suspicious. The coincidences adding up with Mangum were staggering. It was making it a mathematical impossibility that what happened was an accident.

And then, near the end of the two-hour deposition, came the big moment.

My lawyer: "In regard to rear-ending my client's vehicle, do you take full responsibility?"

Mangum goes quiet. He looks down. He looks sullen.

Ten seconds pass. Long seconds.

Mangum: "I do, I just don't agree with it."

Immediately after the car wreck, Mangum and Wadman had accepted 100 percent liability. *Of course* he had to take full responsibility for the wreck. I didn't even have to pay my deductible. He initially agreed to everything that happened when I reported it to my insurance.

My lawyer: "What do you mean you don't agree with it?"

Mangum: "The lawsuit, the damages to his car, I don't agree with it."

When asked if he thought that I could have been physically injured in the wreck, you could see a low-grade boil darken Mangum's face.

He looked agitated. "I'd rather not comment on it," he said.

My lawyer: "Does that upset you?"

Mangum: "It does."

My lawyer: "Why does it upset you?"

Mangum: "This minor of an accident, compared to what I do every day of my life, which is work my butt off—hard—raise my kids and my grandsons every day of my life. This is total bullshit. I've seen my daughter whip my grandkids harder than I bumped that car, and that's how I feel about it."

Mangum was trying to paint a picture that I deliberately braked for some frivolous lawsuit. If that was the case, I would have called the ambulance right then and there, and I would not have waited over a month before I sought medical help. My own actions proved I was more interested in moving forward in life than wanting to get involved in litigation.

Mangum was asked if it would surprise him to learn that I felt he deliberately rear-ended me. He did not let the question finish before he said "Sure." When this information was given to Mangum, he went from looking menacing to looking like a crumpled-up old man. Suddenly, he appeared very frail and very worried.

Any lawyer could see that it wouldn't be a good idea to take this case to court.

After the deposition, my attorney, Tracy Eglet, called up Mangum's attorneys and ripped into them. Mangum's attorney proposed we mediate. As a result, we entered negotiations for a settlement a few days later.

. . . .

Before we started mediation, there was a tragic car accident that was the top news story in Las Vegas for many days. The accident was caused by Scott Gragson, a prominent real estate broker with Colliers International. At the time of the crash, Gragson was Executive Vice President of the Las Vegas Land Division.

You may recall Gragson's name. When I first met Mike Levin at Farbod Sattari's house (the day I kicked Levin out of Sattaris' house, when I didn't know his notorious reputation), Levin was pitching Farbod to buy property owned by Gragson.

Scott Gragson was the grandson of Oran K. Gragson, who served as Mayor of Las Vegas from 1959 to 1974. He was also the father of Noah Gragson, who races for NASCAR in the Xfinity series. He was very well known. He had been involved in many charities and served on the board of directors for Candlelighters, Las Vegas Fire and Rescue Foundation, and Big Brothers and Big Sisters of Southern Nevada.

In surveillance video taken before the crash, Gragson could be seen arguing with a security guard at the gate of a private community. He was leading an entourage of cars from a golf charity event, an event that had been organized by Colliers. Gragson wanted all the cars in his group to come through the gate with him. The guard, however, wanted to check IDs. Gragson got in a shouting match and drove off, clearly in anger. Investigators would later determine the vehicle was going 80 miles per hour in a residential area.

Gragson, who had been drinking at the golf tournament, lost control of his Range Rover. A 36-year-old woman sitting in the back seat was ejected from the car and died at the scene. Two other men were seriously injured. One, a real estate executive named Christopher Bentley, had brain damage. A third man had minor injuries. The woman who died was Melissa Newton. She was the mother of three young daughters. Gragson was arrested on the spot for DUI; his blood-alcohol level was twice the legal limit. The sensational accident touched the entire community—especially those in real estate who knew Gragson and, of course, all the friends and family of Melissa Newton.

To me, the accident was deeply moving. I cried about how I was able to come back after dying and that she was not. Why would God allow me to come back without having a family of my own, and yet she dies and leaves behind three young daughters? This was completely unfair. She deserved to come back a lot more than I did.

I knew I needed to do something, so I donated $3,000 to a GoFundMe campaign for Melissa Newton's family. With the extra fee, the total donation came to $3,300.

That very same night, I hammered out a deal with Kay Roohani—Farbod Sattari's big nemesis. That deal closed five days later, and I took a commission check of $33,000, precisely ten times as much as my modest donation to the family of Melissa Newton. I felt as if the universe was saying thanks for my kindness. However, I knew no amount of money would ease the heartbreak around the tragic loss of this young mother. I also knew that Gragson's deep pockets would likely take care of Melissa Newton's family, but it felt good to do something.

By the way, the accident cost Gragson and his insurance company $21 million—at least. That settlement was with attorneys representing Newton's three children. Most of that would be paid, personally, by

Gragson. Gragson, who pled guilty to the charges in February 2020, was ultimately sentenced to eight to twenty years in prison.

. . . .

My heart was still heavy, thinking about this horrible crash and the senseless loss of life, when we entered mediation a few days later. Mangum's attorneys did not offer much.

They did not understand how anyone could get as hurt as me and still function. I told the judge handling the mediation that the reason I was successful was because I never stopped believing in myself. The judge grinned from ear to ear, and as a result, they made the offer to settle.

It was an offer I took.

It was during the mediation they called Mike Gonzales as a witness who knew me before and after the wreck. I called Mike Gonzales after he left my office and told him everything, including my near-death experience, the voice of God, and my suspicions. I offered to bet him my $1000 to his $100 that my car wreck was not an accident—he said he would never take that bet. He said he would be a character witness if and when it came time to settle. When it was time, he refused to participate. If he would have cooperated, I would have received significantly more money. Mike Gonzales also became really upset when he found out they settled for one million dollars.

I would *refuse* far more money than that if I could get my old professional life back, if I could get back to the income level I had enjoyed prior to the car wreck, if I could not have that perpetual feeling of shock.

I wasn't going to say no. I also was not going to drag out my litigation any longer than I needed to. Murder attempts are not supposed to be in the civil courts for insurance to settle; they are supposed to be investigated criminally and are for the criminal courts.

I agreed to the settlement offer, but I had to protect myself from others that might have been involved. I signed an informal settlement agreement at the mediation. A week later, they sent over the formal agreement and asked for a universal settlement, meaning that every person on the planet was excluded from any type of possible future litigation over my car wreck. They also asked for a confidentiality clause. They tried to sneak that into the formal agreement, but my attorney caught it and said such a clause would cost them another $9 million. They pulled it off the table.

The universal exclusion would mean I could never go after the Sattaris or Mike Levin for any involvement in this case. At the time, I had not yet begun my investigation. I was only looking to settle my car wreck, so I didn't have various other people on my radar.

I told the lawyers that the settlement would have to exclude the Sattari Family, Omega Family Limited Partnership, and Mike Levin. This was on a Friday. I heard back the following Tuesday that they couldn't give me the exclusions in case these parties were affiliated with Wadman Corporation. I raised hell about the possible affiliation, my attorney attacked them, and they finally granted the exclusions.

After they agreed, their attorney reached out to my attorney and said they wouldn't give me the $1 million if I was going to go to law enforcement. I told my attorney to tell their attorney I needed the exclusions for a possible commission dispute, and they finally relented.

I had come so far. I had gone through the long process of discovery and the depositions. I couldn't just turn around and walk away from a settlement. I told them I was *not* going to go to law enforcement.

At the time, at least, that statement was true.

CHAPTER 25

Forgiveness in My Heart

I t was about a month after the settlement that I was looking to sue the Sattari family through civil courts—for fraud and for stealing documents out of my office. I had plenty of material to bring a lawsuit.

Out of the blue, Mordred emailed me to ask for a meeting. Mordred claimed the state real estate division needed a form signed that would validate his work history. A minute later, to establish credibility for his request, Mordred's office manager emailed me asking me to sign the same form. He also wanted me to meet with Mordred in person. This was a bizarre request. I could see Mordred was behind it. After things were revealed about the driver of the truck, the last thing I wanted to do was interact with Mordred.

Something strange was going on. What did Mordred want me to sign? And for what reason? Why did he want to meet me? What was the real reason for *that*?

I believe Farbod got a tip that I was getting ready to try and sue.

That's why his son attempted to meet with me—perhaps to threaten me in person.

That's when I started nagging the FBI.

I called their 800 number. I was very persistent. It took me almost a dozen calls to get through to a real person who took interest in my story, but I pursued criminal investigation of the Sattaris the way I would pursue a land deal. I was relentless. I was a pit bull.

One time, I accidentally let it slip that I had died and come back to life.

"You died?" said the FBI agent. "You died and came back?" I told her that was true. "Then there's no need to investigate," she said, and hung up.

Getting the FBI officially involved was, to say the least, a difficult task.

Finally, I got a female agent on the line who took down a lot of details. I started with the violent car collision and how it was made to look like an accident. I told her about all the coincidences that were behind the wreck. I told her about the deal I was supposed to broker and the money I was about to make. I told her that I believed one of their own was behind the wreck—former FBI agent and former federal prisoner Mike Levin. *That* got their attention. At first, I focused only on the Sattari family situation. I didn't mention the pig farm loan initially. I didn't have all the dots connected yet on the pig farm. The pig farm was out of sight and out of mind because I had settled that case in 2018.

I realized that since the summer of 2018, when I fired Farbod Sattari, I had carried anger in my heart. I wanted to get rid of it. I decided to extend an olive branch.

On September 11, 2019—an important day, to be sure, and a day of forgiveness for many—I emailed Farbod.

The only reason I reached out to Farbod was because the lady at the FBI who took the complaint begged me to sue them and not let them get away with it. I decided on a more peaceful approach. I would never have engaged Farbod if not for the insistence of the FBI wanting me to go after him.

I emailed Farbod an invoice for the $480,000 I was supposed to get paid on Hualapai and Farm and one for the $48,000 I was owed on S. Las Vegas Blvd and Richmar, which he promised to pay if I ever fired him as a client.

It is true Richmond paid me $80,000, but it was a far cry from the

$480,000 Farbod was going to pay me to teach his son the ropes. Farbod Sattari replied two days later—on all days, Friday the 13th.

When I received Farbod's email the first time, I skipped right to the end. That's how PTSD works. If something or someone gives me the creeps, I block it or them out. I couldn't read the whole email.

Many, many months later, I finally read his entire message. Farbod Sattari's claims were, of course, preposterous. Farbod made some outrageous claims; Farbod tried to claim my brain injury was from the Southwest Airlines incident, which no doctor ever diagnosed me with. Farbod tried to say I wanted him to pretend it was from the car wreck. I never once mentioned my Southwest Airlines incident ever with Farbod. Did his attorney get my transcripts from the deposition or did the FBI investigate me for taking a million-dollar payout hoping to catch me lying about past injuries? Farbod had signed a letter of intent with D.R. Horton right before my car wreck. He also gave me the listing on Hualapai and Farm in March of 2017, right after he went into escrow with Mike Levin behind my back, not March of 2016, like he claimed in the email. Immediately following the car wreck, he backed out of the transaction with D.R. Horton after he signed a letter of intent with them.

That night, without reading his entire email, I called Farbod. I was nervous picking up the phone. But I wanted to patch things up. I wanted the money he owed me. I really didn't want to end up in litigation over it. I wanted to settle this businessman to businessman. The FBI thought I should take my case through civil courts, but I was determined to work things out peacefully.

To my surprise, Farbod started chatting as if we were old friends. He wanted us to grab lunch. I agreed.

A few days later, we met for lunch at the Bagel Café. It was a Saturday. I got there first and sat in a two-person booth near the front of the restaurant. I was feeling unsettled.

I hadn't seen Farbod in about fourteen months. When he arrived, Farbod was complaining about his poor health. He always had a big Buddha belly. He had always complained about issues with his prostate, always going into too much detail.

I ordered a spinach and feta omelet and a sun-dried bagel with Nova Lox cream cheese. I don't remember what Farbod ordered.

What I do remember is that I laid everything out. Everything. My complete testament of God. The whole nine yards. I told him what happened to me. I told him about the voice of God.

When I told him about the driver of the pickup trying to assault me, Farbod asked about it several times.

He asked whether I had mentioned the attempted assault in the deposition, and I told him I had.

"You shouldn't have done that," he said.

He was starting to understand the power I had over him. He looked worried and fearful.

When I was done walking him through the whole story and what had happened to me, he started treating me like a long-lost family member. He started talking about how the whole family missed me. He started complaining about how I had disappeared, and about the events that led to the moment we had parted ways.

We talked about a lot of the events that led up to when I fired Omega Family Limited Partnership as a client. We also talked about the strange buyer who was allegedly going to purchase Patrick and I-215. The one who wanted me to meet him at the property late at night. The one who always texted me on burner phones, who stopped texting me once I mentioned it was Mike Levin on the other end of the text messages.

And he told me I was smart not to meet with Mordred in July when he had tried to get me to sign papers in person.

"That was smart," he said, referring to the meeting I had avoided at all costs. "That boy is a violent person."

I got the message loud and clear—I should be afraid. This comment by Farbod matched up with what he told me shortly after I had fired the Sattaris. At the time, he told me I must "fear The Mordred." Over and over.

Farbod told me that Mordred had recently broken up with a girlfriend. The girlfriend had ended the relationship, Farbod explained, because of Mordred's streaks of violence.

"Why does that not surprise me?" I said to Farbod.

Farbod shrugged it off.

Again, Farbod wanted to intimidate me. I recalled that about a month before I fired him, Mordred had asked me if I parked both of my cars in the garage at night. My intuition was that he was trying to find out if he could plant a tracer on my car so he could keep tabs on me.

I told Farbod that I thought Mike Levin must have been behind the whole car wreck—*and he agreed with me.* Mike Levin! A former federal felon, a former FBI agent. Creepy Mike Levin. A man who knew so many outright criminals. A man who had made a career out of his network of formal federal prisoners.

It was likely a moment of weakness for Farbod, to openly admit that Mike was likely right in the middle of the whole scheme that led to the attempt on my life. Farbod first admitted to Mike Levin's involvement right when I went into litigation, which led me to fire him as a client. It came back to me right before I fired Farbod, his words, "Mike Levin has never heard of you ever again and you have never heard of him in your federal court case."

I told him how the situation with the pig farm was most assuredly also behind the wreck. I somehow knew my murder had to do with more than just Hualapai and Farm. I felt it was connected to the loan I made to Bob Combs as well.

Farbod changed the subject. He didn't want to talk about it. It was clear he was being evasive.

But that is who Farbod thought he was; he thought he could tell you something dark, and that you wouldn't have the power to do anything about it.

Farbod Sattari loved how his vast wealth gave him this type of power. Poor people could not get away with the crap that this web of characters was trying to put over on me.

Yes, I could have gotten up right then and left.

But I was in interrogation mode. I wanted to know more. I wanted answers. And, of course, I wanted my money.

I came to the conclusion my wreck had also to do with the loan I made to Bob Combs. My wreck happened 12 days before Mike Montandon was announced as the broker of the pig farm and contiguous acreage. Why would Bob Combs go into escrow with someone fresh out of prison that owed the IRS millions of dollars? Shawn Lampman flipped out of the escrow for one million dollars, same amount I settled my car wreck for. I reflected on how my collateral was tampered one month after the assault to defraud me out of the loan. I thought of the time in the pig farm deposition when his wife claimed Bob bought pigs with the money and they all died of a virus. I also reflected on the times Farbod, Mordred, and Nahid would taunt me about felons harassing them who were looking for me, like they were giving me a profound clue for me to solve.

Now speaking to Farbod I mentioned how I thought the car wreck was about the loan I made to Bob Combs.

Suddenly, Farbod started talking about how much his whole family missed me. Again. He started mentioning his health again. He was very good at playing the victim, just as he had played the victim with his health when I first fired him.

Out of the blue, Farbod told me he and Nahid had recently been in a couple of fender-benders—and that *they* were being sued over the crashes.

Right. Sure.

I knew what Farbod was doing; he was trying to portray that karma had already been served. I took his stories about their fender-benders with a grain of salt. Farbod Sattari is the father of lies and half-truths. I didn't buy it.

I kept wanting to bring the conversation around to the commission he owed me, but he kept changing the subject. Finally, he said he would "consider" paying me a commission, and he left it at that.

He walked me to my car. Of course, I had paid the check. He never offered.

Outside, we talked again about what he owed me, and again, he left a carrot dangling that he would "possibly" pay me.

Out of the blue, he offered to give me a few listings to sell. *Give me a break.* Did he think I would fall for that? Just because he agreed to *list* a parcel to sell meant absolutely nothing about his willingness to *sell*. To close a deal. He was stringing me along. He was buying time. He was trying to get his hooks into me. By this point, I knew how he operated. I wasn't going down that road again.

I showed him my new Range Rover, and he started giving me grief. He claimed I would be a "target" driving around in such a nice car.

"Somebody could just stab you in the neck with a knife and take the car," he said. He did a quick stabbing gesture at my neck. "You'd be dead, and your car would be gone."

How freaking creepy.

· · · ·

In October 2019, I decided to return to kenpo karate. I knew there were many loose strings out there that needed to be tied up, but I also wanted to get back to doing the things I enjoyed.

I ran into Kimberly Toy. You'll recall Kimberly. She had been a big part of my life in the months leading up to the wreck. A couple of days before my car wreck, we had that disagreement over what to watch on Netflix, and she stormed out of the house. Six weeks later, in March 2016, I saw her again, and she witnessed the toll that the wreck had taken on my body. While she was empathetic about what had happened to me, she also made it clear that we were not getting back together.

In 2019, she was still at kenpo karate. She often took her brother's kids to the dojo to watch them train. This time, she was the one who had changed. She was using a portable oxygen system. Of course, it was impossible to miss. Chatting with her, she explained that she needed the oxygen device for a lung infection she was fighting. I told her that I hoped she would feel better soon, and then I went into detail about my near-death experience. We talked about the motives behind the wreck and all my suspicions, and she told me one thing:

"Always trust your intuition."

This was something we had talked about at length when we dated.

When I was at Nevada Community Enrichment Center I learned that brain injuries amplify what you already have going on. My intuition was really sharp before my death but upon my returned it became amplified in the form of PTSD. I told her that it had never failed me after I died.

It was great to see Kimberly again. We chatted off and on. We would always exchange some words for a few minutes whenever we saw each other at kenpo karate. But then in November 2019, I stopped going to the dojo and stopped running into Kimberly.

I didn't know it at the time, but I would never see her again.

. . . .

Two months earlier, another woman had come into my life. Her name was Jane. I'd known her since 2003—a beautiful person with gorgeous emerald eyes and a very appealing allure. I had no idea at the time, of course, that her return to my world would lead to a major confession from a key player behind my car wreck.

In October 2019, after we had been living together for a couple of months, Jane confided in me that in March of 2017, she had been in a moped wreck in Thailand, where she had been living. An ex-boyfriend, she said, had tried to murder her in a jealous rage. He chased her down and ran her off the road. After three days of being unconscious, she woke up in the hospital, and her ex-boyfriend was sitting there. She woke up screaming bloody murder. Security staff took her ex-boyfriend away.

I immediately felt a connection to Jane when she told me this. Here she was in a violent motor wreck, much like mine, and she had suffered a traumatic brain injury too.

And it was *attempted murder, just like my wreck.*

I immediately felt a desire to protect her. I wanted to love her and take care of her. I did not see it as a coincidence. I saw it as God bringing us together for a powerful reason.

Jane told me that another ex-boyfriend named Shawn Lampman gave her no financial help after the moped wreck. I told her that would never happen with me.

I had a distinct feeling that Elohim was bringing me and Jane together for some divine purpose.

I was super happy to have her in my life. It wasn't until long after she moved in with me that I found out Shawn Lampman was the straw buyer on the pig farm. Then, the pieces of the puzzle really started to fall into place, because Shawn Lampman and Jane were also acquainted. Jane was Lampman's ex-girlfriend.

Lampman had received his real estate license around three months *after* my car wreck. I am told by another land broker that Lampman flipped out of the pig farm deal for the exact same amount I settled my car wreck for—$1 million.

When I first heard this, I was stunned. It felt as if God gave me Jane as a gift, to help me better understand the conspiracy behind the attempt to take my life.

I was 100 percent done with my car wreck, but it appeared that God was telling me there was more to uncover.

I loved Jane much more than she loved me. I did everything in my power to make her happy. I spent tens of thousands of dollars on her for clothes and household items. She had virtually nothing when she came back to the United States from Thailand, only one change of clothes. I helped her start a company that sold jewelry made in Thailand. I paid off her credit card debts.

The first sign that things were not going well was when I was at my second home in Austin. She was supposed to be dog-sitting for me, and I noticed she was sneaking out around 8:00 p.m. and then coming back at 8:00 a.m. This horrified me, as I love my dogs; I did not want them to damage their kidneys because Jane wanted to have a fling with someone and didn't take them outside often enough. My dogs are Labradors and are not used to being at home alone all night. In fact, they had not once ever been home all night alone.

I had but two requests for Jane. One was for her to please be there for my animals when I was out of town. The second request was to not hang out with Shawn Lampman. When I found out Jane ignored the first request, I was devastated and hurt.

I immediately booked a flight from Austin back home to Las Vegas. I walked into my house. Jane, of course, was startled to see me. I told her

I was upset because she had abandoned my animals. I was also upset that she was seeing someone else, but I did not tell her this. I know in relationships that love is not always equal both ways. This was the case with us. I loved Jane unconditionally, and she did not return that love.

It was a couple of days after coming home from Austin that I asked her to move out of my house. I did not feel like I was kicking her out on the streets. She had other options, including other family members.

Right before I kicked her out, she asked for a ride to go visit her girlfriend, Lela. In the car, she told me that she had a threesome with her girlfriend, Lela, and her ex-boyfriend, Shawn Lampman. I freaked out. I could not believe she had seen Shawn. It was part of the reason I asked her to leave. You see the thing is, I was starting to suspect Shawn was somehow connected to my murder. I could not live with a person who was seeing someone I thought tried to have me killed. It was all too much for me to deal with.

I told her if she wanted only friendship from me, she could date anyone on this earth other than Shawn. I did not want him in my life. It was the one thing I asked besides taking care of my animals.

The fact that Shawn was the straw buyer on the pig farm did not sit right with me. There were too many coincidences with Shawn and my violent wreck. I felt Elohim tugging me towards the pig farm situation. I had settled my lawsuit over the car wreck and wanted to move on with my life. Elohim, I would soon come to realize, had other things in mind. The big confession was yet to come. I reflected on all the times Mordred, Farbod, and Nahid were claiming they were harassed by criminals, always throwing off clues to those behind my murder. Now I was suspecting two felons behind the wreck: Mike Levin and Shawn Lampman.

. . . .

During the fall of 2019, following our meeting at the Bagel Café, Farbod Sattari and I communicated two or three times a month. The conversations didn't amount to much, and they certainly didn't lead to him paying what he owed me.

One thing Farbod did not know was that in April 2019, I had started putting out feelers to see if I could land a job with an established real estate company. I was quite sure that if I got into a legal battle with Farbod Sattari, the first thing he would do would be to countersue and come after my real estate company. I wanted to make sure there was nothing there for Farbod to pursue if it came to that.

I tried to get on with Colliers International. The timing wasn't right. One of the executives got the impression that I wanted to take over Scott Gragson's spot, but that wasn't the case at all.

Then, I got a call out of the blue from a guy named David, who was a managing broker at an international firm. He offered me a job. It felt like a ton of bricks was lifted from my shoulders. I immediately started the process of winding down my company.

Suddenly, I was working with a family of twenty or thirty good real estate brokers. I had a big team to collaborate with. I had tools to access data all over the world. I was working in a top-flight firm.

The firm gave me ownership in the company and offered incredible benefits—medical, dental, life insurance, and long-term disability too. I had a nice office in a spiffy building in Summerlin, the development that was started by Howard Hughes (who bought 25,000 acres on the western edge of Las Vegas in the early 1950s for about $3 an acre).

Like the neighborhood where I lived, the office space was classy. More importantly, landing with this firm meant that Farbod Sattari had nothing to come after in terms of business assets under my name if we ended up in litigation with one another. I became a broker at a highly regarded, international real estate firm.

CHAPTER 26

Apology and Voice of God Proven

As 2019 drew to a close, I wanted to wrap things up too. I wanted closure. I hated how the business with Farbod Sattari was dragging on and on.

In December, I texted Farbod and told him I wanted to put this commission business behind me; that I wanted what he owed me.

He called me back, but I missed the call.

So, I called him again.

And I got the same old Farbod Sattari, the guy who threatened my life when I fired him in 2015. Farbod started threatening me again. He told me that he was friends with the district attorney and that he was going to have me arrested.

When he started going into the tirade, I told Farbod what happened to me on February 10, 2016. He started listening to my story. At first, he didn't understand that my story had to do with my car wreck. I told him everything—about being in the afterlife. Everything. I gave him my complete testament of God. I tried to put the fear of God in him, but he couldn't be frightened. Nothing changed. He continued his attack. The threats started escalating from there. He threatened me for an hour.

This was startling because it had been a long time since he had behaved in such a harsh manner. The last time he had done this was before the wreck, nearly four years earlier.

Farbod Sattari went on to say many disparaging things about me. I told him about the confession Jessamine gave me about her brother—that she told me Mordred tried to have me killed three times. She said he had the means of doing it, and he knew the people who would get it done, describing the driver perfectly.

And then Farbod started giggling like a little girl.

"See," I said, "you even think this is funny."

Then Farbod started taunting me that the wife George, the former agent of mine, wanted to sue me for how I ran my business. She is an attorney in Las Vegas, Nevada

"Is that so?" I asked. "I just saw George for the first time in years at Drysdale Jiu-Jitsu, and the next day someone called me looking for him. That's no coincidence."

Farbod told me that his attorney, Roger Crow, told the FBI that I orchestrated my entire car wreck, and that I had a previous brain injury I had covered up from a Southwest Airlines accident. The Southwest Airlines accident hurt my neck, not my brain. I would later read his email after this incident and find him referencing my Southwest Airlines injury in the email for the first time. Then, he started telling me about all the nice things he had done for me, and how he was the "number one witness" for my doctors in the lawsuit over my car wreck. Then, he caught himself. It didn't make sense. How could he have testified on my behalf in a lawsuit over the wreck, and at the same time, go along with the fabrication his attorney gave to the FBI?

"Are you recording me?" he screamed.

"Of course not, I wouldn't do that," I said.

He hung up.

I called him right back—I still wanted to work out this commission business.

He answered right away.

He told me that if the dispute ever went to the civil courts, he knew he would lose. He added, "It will never get there because I will kill you first!"

"Farbod, what does Mike Levin think of me turning him into the FBI?" I asked.

Farbod Sattari started screaming at me.

"He is going to kill you. He is going to kill you! You are going to die so quick you won't know what happened."

I started laughing.

"Farbod," I said. "That already happened to me in the shopping center parking lot."

Click. I hung up the phone.

Farbod Sattari did get his point across, and his threats and warnings certainly convinced me that he could carry out his death threats. I never did sue him in civil court. I am always able to, as there is no statute of limitation for fraud, but I choose to have a more peaceful existence.

. . . .

In early 2020, I started gathering information for this book. I knew I needed to capture in writing everything I knew and everything I had experienced.

This book is my attempt to put in narrative form exactly what happened to me and what I experienced, particularly while I was dead, and my experience when I came back to this earth. I know many people have experienced this—crossing over into death and coming back. It's eerie that many of us say we saw the same lights, had the same feelings about seeing all of time, and hearing the voice of God.

I decided that I needed to hold those behind the wreck accountable for their actions, so I started putting together complaints against the shady individuals who I felt were behind my murder. In the end, my lawyer and I did not file those complaints with the Nevada real estate division until early 2021. It took time for a few more pieces to fall into place, including Shawn Lampman's role in the pig farm deal.

In March 2020, I felt a powerful urge to reconnect with Jane. I didn't like the way things had ended with her. I also had a powerful feeling that something would come out of reconnecting with her.

A couple of months after I began writing this book—as an attempt to commit to paper everything I knew about the car wreck and everything that happened to me before, during, and after—I got a notice in the mail that Jane's dog Dora had an appointment coming up at the vet. The notice had come to my home address, but Jane was no longer living there.

I called Jane on FaceTime to tell her that I would take care of the bill. You know by now how much I love dogs, and of course, I loved Jane. I was emotional at the time as I'd just lost my grandmother three days before, and really wanted someone to talk to.

It was March 28, 2020.

When she answered, she told me she was hanging out at the Oasis RV Park. She introduced another guy that was with her as "Art from Howard & Howard."

She told me that Art looked like her ex-boyfriend.

And right there on FaceTime, Art started ripping into me. *Very strange.* He started criticizing me for all the nice things I had done for Jane. He was being a total jerk. It was very clear that this guy was displaying some sort of jealousy towards me and seemed more than just Jane's friend.

"Why did you do all these things for Jane?" Art would ask.

"Because I loved her and wanted to settle down and have a family with her," I said.

There was another woman and another guy with them as well. Jane told me they'd been doing mushrooms, which must have been acting like truth serum because Art was being extremely blunt. He was a menacing-looking guy, big and kind of balding with reddish hair.

I tried to change the subject to the book I was writing. I started going through some of the details about the wreck. I finally told Art I thought I was murdered over the Bob Combs loan.

"Have you ever heard of the pig farm?" I asked.

"No, I've never heard of it," said Art.

"You told me you've lived here your whole life, and you've never heard of the pig farm?"

"No, I've never heard of the pig farm."

And that's when I started to give him my testament of God—all the details from the car wreck. I had a hunch this guy called Art was actually Shawn Lampman. I probably would not have gone into so much detail if I didn't have this hunch.

Suddenly, Art became standoffish. Distant. I then got to the part of the story where I told them about the wailing sound that came out of my mouth when I died.

The man started laughing like the Joker from *Batman*, but high on mushrooms. "Make that wailing noise again," he said, "I want to hear it."

He laughed some more.

"How can I make that noise if you only make it upon death?" I asked.

Again, the hysterical laughter. That was when I hung up.

One minute later, I received a video message. Art sat there in his chair in the RV at the Oasis.

"Michael, this is Art. I was a fucking dick. I'm sorry. Genuinely sorry for what I did, what I said. It was offensive. I know it was. I hope you'll forgive me. For my dick-fucken move. That's all I gotta say."

A quick check of Google told me that the man introduced as Art was, in fact, Shawn Lampman, the former federal felon. Same short hair. Big guy. Intimidating presence.

When he sent the apology, the first thing he apologized for was everything he had done to me and, as an afterthought, he apologized for everything he had said to me. Why mention both?

I knew right then and there it wasn't an apology for what he had said to me or how he had mocked me. This was an apology for the car wreck.

I could feel it deep down in my bones.

Around the same time I received the creepy apology, I ended up with a new client who, ironically, along with some others, had lost over 18 million to Shawn Lampman (Case. A-11-651042-C). In the lawsuit, Lampman raised money for thousands of acres of land in Albuquerque, New Mexico. They never ended up with the property and were duped out of their money. The only reason why they lost the lawsuit was because their client's attorney did not file the paperwork on time. I truly felt powerful forces to be at work.

. . . .

Toward the end of March 2020, I started texting Kimberly Toy to see how she was doing. I would go out with her if she was up for it. I also wanted to possibly broker a parcel of land she and Robert Sigler had purchased near the location of the new stadium for the Las Vegas Raiders.

I texted her repeatedly.

No response.

I started calling Kimberly, leaving her messages.

Again, no response. I thought that was strange. We weren't dating, but I considered her a good friend.

I went to kenpo karate two months later and ran into Robert Sigler.

"Where is my friend Kimberly?" I asked.

Robert told me that Kimberly died on March 19, 2020. Supposedly, she died in her sleep.

I was in shock and horrified. I felt all the wind taken out of me. Here I was texting her about selling her land and rekindling our relationship—and she had left the earth.

I went home and was really saddened. Why would she die, and yet I was allowed to come back after being murdered?

It was not fair. I felt that if the wreck had never happened, she would possibly still be alive.

I was distressed.

March of 2020 was a rough month for me. I lost a good friend, Kimberly Toy, on March 19, and I lost my beloved grandmother, Florence, six days later, on March 25. Both deaths were devastating, even though I didn't learn about Kimberly's death until two months after she passed. And then on March 28—the confession and apology about the car wreck in the video from "Art" (a.k.a. Shawn Lampman) at the Oasis RV Park.

The news of Kimberly's death shook me to my core. I found myself praying all night for my beloved friend's soul—that she be given a seat next to God in the afterlife.

I didn't sleep one second that night.

Had we not had that argument over Netflix, I knew everything would have been different, and that our lives would have gone in different directions. Both of our lives.

The car wreck delayed my reaching out way back in 2016 and, as a result, she had gone her own way. It was the car wreck that took her from me—on February 10, 2016—and not the sudden death on March 19, 2020.

Do I blame myself? No. I blame those behind the car wreck.

The attempt on my life.

· · · ·

After I was given the video apology, and the whole world went into the pandemic lockdown, I reached out to Robert Drysdale. I started training with purpose in private sessions in jiu-jitsu. I had reached out to Jeff Speakman also, but he was in quarantine like the rest of the world. I trained like a beast during lockdown, getting my ass kicked daily by Drysdale. He knew the neck crunches saved my life when I was murdered, and he would always remind me to do them daily.

The ass-kicking went on for ninety days, and then I earned my blue belt in jiu-jitsu a week before they released the whole world from quarantine—in June 2020. It was a great accomplishment, and it felt good.

Right after I became a blue belt, a new student arrived; he asked me about my belt and all my training, including my ten years as a white belt. I told him about my broken jaw that had slowed me down from getting a blue belt, and I told him about my car wreck, made to look like an accident, that was meant to kill me and slowed me down for over three years. He immediately became intrigued.

"Tell me about the car wreck," he said.

With him, like I do with so many other people, I gave him my testament of God.

He immediately told me that he had a similar near-death experience, and that he worked for the D.A.'s office. He told me he was at a robbery, sitting in his squad car in a private parking lot, when somebody rear-ended him traveling at a speed of 80 miles per hour. The only reason he lived is that the driver's bumper went underneath his bumper and took away much of the impact. The wreck sounded astronomically deadlier than mine with the speeds involved. I could tell my new friend was protected by powerful forces that had brought us together.

We both thought this was profound on a cosmic scale. I started working with him, giving him many documentations tying many people to my car wreck. He created a spider web of those that conspired to murder me. The spider web included Mark Peplowski, Bob Combs, Mike Montandon, Jim Zeiter, Shawn Lampman, Ray Ghouli, Farbod Sattari, Mordred Sattari, Benjamin Troy Mangum, and Mike Levin.

My new friend and ally told me that a detective friend was investigating the pig farm deal tied to my car wreck. It looked like my complaint to the FBI really got their attention.

Whereas before I felt all alone, I now felt God was protecting me on a divine scale. I was happy to have this new ally in my life.

Towards the end of 2020, my new friend was assaulted by a gunman. He managed to grapple the weapon out of his attacker's hand, using jiu-jitsu to fend off the deadly assault. As a result, he was promoted to detective.

· · · ·

Throughout 2020, I kept working on this book and seeing the pieces come together. When I looked back and saw how everything fit—and all the coincidences I could no longer ignore—it was easy to see the big picture.

In February 2021, I had compiled enough information that I took five complaints to the state real estate division—one complaint each for Shawn Lampman, Ray Ghouli, Mike Levin, Mike Montandon, and Jim Zeiter. I went after the people who I felt were connected to my murder. I did not go after the Sattaris in the complaint to the real estate division. I did give the Nevada real estate division the goofy contract Mike Levin and Mordred negotiated behind my back where he gets his earnest money back and keeps the escrow open on a property Farbod owned.

I told the real estate division about some of the coincidences that made it an impossibility for my car wreck not to be attempted murder. I also explained all of the coincidences that linked each of these people, plus, the too-convenient timing of certain properties being pulled off the market, and my collateral being defrauded.

I filed the complaints on February 4, 2021—six days before the five-year anniversary of my death. I also sent a copy to my new secret ally inside law enforcement.

The real estate division gave me receipts for the complaints on February 18, 2021. That same day, I received an email from Janet Combs (Bob Combs' wife) asking me to remove them from my email distribution list.

Right after complaints were filed, Ray Ghouli emailed me to ask for the price of a new 3.11-acre property I had listed across from Mandalay Bay on Las Vegas Boulevard. I emailed back the price.

One week later, Ray Ghouli had his attorney call my attorney, the one who helped me with the complaint. He was fishing for information. The first question Ghouli's attorney asked my attorney over the phone was: "*What*—does this guy have a brain injury?"

They were hoping my attorney would admit to something like that so they could use it in their counter-response. When I was a member and later a volunteer at NCEP, the first thing they taught me was that when you have a brain injury, there are unsavory people who will always try to use that against you. Had my attorney said I had a traumatic brain injury, they would try to claim I was nuts as a result, without knowing the facts.

. . . .

Licensees in Nevada are required to hold on to closing documents for five years, and there were only eight months remaining before the five-year anniversary of the closing of the pig farm. I was running out of time.

I wanted to make sure I filed my complaints to the division before the five-year mark of my murder; I didn't want the division to be able to say that they couldn't investigate it due to my car wreck being over five years old.

Two days after I turned those five people in to the real estate division, I took and passed my second-degree brown belt in kenpo karate. I wouldn't let these people deter me from my goals.

It was in April 2021 that I believed my life was in jeopardy, and I decided to leave town. I told others about the feelings I was having, that if I stayed in town, my life was at stake. The next day, someone called by the name of Nephi, wanting to get into a property I had listed on East Charleston. Nephi informed me that I would be dealing with Mike Montandon, former owner of the pig farm and former FBI agent. Nephi was startled when he found out I lived in Austin, Texas.

Was Montandon really a former FBI agent? It would be the bridge that connected Mike Levin to him. I wanted to email Montandon and ask but held back.

God was not done with me. It was in May 2021 that my client emailed me an offer from Mordred to hammer out. I'd had a recurring dream about Mordred prior to turning everyone in. In the dream, no matter where I went, Mordred followed me. Then, the night before my trip to the real estate division, Mordred called and apologized profusely and begged me not to turn him in. I was so overwhelmed when I had this dream, I decided to leave Mordred out of it.

I did not hammer out that deal with Mordred, but was very professional and emailed him other properties his dad might be interested in. It was then I had another Mordred dream. This one was at my house, and Mike Levin and Mordred were hanging out together on my high-rise balcony. They were asking me to come over and join them. I was totally creeped out. Upon awakening, I decided I'd better not engage with Mordred at all.

The following week, I was hanging out at my house with my girl-friend, and Mordred called me.

"Mike, do you know who this is?"

I heard the laughter I had not heard in years. Mordred started chatting about properties and then asked about my house with the views.

"Oh, that; I am moving," I said. The hairs on the back of my girl-friend's neck immediately went up.

"Mike, I will buy your house, and you can live there until your new house is built," Mordred told me.

It was as if my dream was playing out. He wanted to call me monthly and stay in touch. I could not let him know how badly he creeped me out, so I agreed. "Of course," I said. I never unblocked his phone number. Before this incident, an agent at my new firm emailed me a picture of Mordred brandishing a gun on social media, where he claimed he was going to kill anyone who tried to steal his hand sanitizer. That is one relationship that is forever over!

CHAPTER 27

Case Closed

L ooking back, I reflected on some of the coincidences that show my car wreck was an attempted murder.

In the spring of 2015, Farbod threatened to kill me when I fired him as a client. He also said I will die so quick I won't know what happened.

Bob Combs relentlessly pursued me to change my collateral to a livestock loan after I loaned him a half million dollars. Bob Combs walked me to my car after I loaned him the money and asked me if I wanted to go hunting with him. It was the end of January 2016 when he called me up and said that he decided to hire me as his broker for the pig farm and surrounding parcels of land, but again, I had to convert my collateral to a livestock loan before giving me the listing.

A couple of days before my car wreck, Mordred called me up hysterically screaming that he wanted my lifestyle, as he entered into a violent rage.

Right after the wreck, the driver asked me to commit insurance fraud by saying that I was moving when I reported the incident to my insurance company. When I did not agree, he became violently confrontational. The driver agreed to my version of events when I reported the crash to my insurance but quickly changed his story when he found out I was hurt.

When the car wreck first happened, there was a change in the way Farbod, Nahid, and Mordred treated me. Mordred, for a while, stopped saying people were assaulting him because they were looking for me. Farbod stopped calling me nightly, and I had the willies around Farbod, Mordred, and Nahid. Mordred and Nahid were paid a substantial amount of money in October of 2015, shortly before my car wreck. I had a signed letter of intent with Farbod Sattari and D.R. Horton right before my wreck, but right after, he backed out of the transaction. The day after the car wreck, his business partner Ray Ghouli started to engage me. Farbod then quickly backed out of the deal with D.R. Horton. Ray then signed a letter of intent with D.R. Horton regarding some land he owned, which he, in turn, also retracted.

Mike Montandon was announced in the *Las Vegas Sun* as the broker of the pig farm twelve days after the collision. A month after my car wreck, the collateral Bob Combs gave me was tampered with when he recorded his new living trust on the property, and then that recording was deleted online to hide the transfer. Mike Montandon's colleague, Travis Nelson, came around my office right after my car wreck to relentlessly taunt me about my neck. Mike Montandon worked at Nevada Title while serving as the North Las Vegas mayor. The driver who rear-ended me talked about how I grabbed my neck when I got out of my car in his deposition. It seems like the driver was bragging about how he hurt my neck to those who engaged him to murder me.

Mark Pelowski and Bob Combs sued me at the end of 2016, claiming I was defaming the title when I put in my commission demand, which I did no such thing. In fact, this is what they did to my collateral when they recorded Bob's new trust on the 20 acres Bob put up for collateral when I loaned him a half million dollars and then deceptively covered up by deleting the event online. If I would have taken a deed in lieu of foreclosure then it would have wiped out my loan and I would have been out of a half million dollars. I felt they were trying to protect the driver who tried to murder me by creating a distraction. Shortly after being sued by them, Mark Peplowski got arrested for having sex with prostitutes on Freemont Street, and a prostitute told law enforcement that

Peplowski and her were involved in identity theft. Later in the Comb's litigation, I learned Bob bought pigs with the money I loaned him, and they all died from a virus. His attorney asked if he knew who I was messing with right before Mike Montandon was going to be deposed. He brought up my car wreck while in Combs' litigation, and it felt like he knew something I did not.

In October of 2016, I listed West Wendover for Farbod and Ray, when I felt compelled to talk to Ray about my car wreck. That was when he asked if I could still function and then looked over at Mordred and winked. Ray hated me with a passion after my crash but was kind to me before it. There was a total shift in his demeanor towards me.

In January of 2017, Travis Nelson left me a voicemail, upset my client went into escrow with Prologis, and he did not get it. In the voicemail, he taunted me about my neck. Travis Nelson ended up with the Hualapai and Farm escrow and also the escrow with Combs.

In March of 2017, Farbod went into escrow with Mike Levin on his property located at Craig and Allen, where the buyer got his earnest money back after 30 days with the escrow remaining open. I felt it was a payback. Mike Levin acted like he did something to me when he engaged me during the escrow. He then tried to get me to commit a criminal act by signing on behalf of Farbod. Levin threw off the willies, so much I had to block him from contacting me.

When I entered litigation, Mordred said felons were assaulting him and looking for me. Nahid claimed a felon helped her load her groceries in her car in Boca Park and started asking about me. Farbod claimed he was being assaulted by felons at Wahoo Tacos because they wanted to know where I lived. I feel they were giving me powerful clues about who was behind my car wreck.

In the summer of 2018, I got a text message from a buyer Farbod and Mordred referred to me, right after I went into litigation on Sattari's land at Patrick and 215, claiming Farbod wanted to pay me a 6% commission on a 20 million escrow. The buyer wanted to meet me at the property at 9:30 at night. The phone number was a burner phone (305-707-3691). I mention the number, as I was told the government is able to find out who purchased burner phones ever since the catastrophe of 9/11. When I mentioned to Farbod and Mordred that I felt the buyer was Mike Levin, Mordred called me the next morning at 6:30, incredibly nervous, and began trying to talk me out of what I thought of the buyer. At 7:30, Mordred called my office and hysterically threatened my assistant and me. Farbod called me up and said Mike Levin has never heard of you ever again and you have never heard of him in your federal litigation. Farbod was trying to say Mike Levin was done picking away at your life as long as you don't bring him up in your federal car wreck case. The day after Mordred assaulted my assistant and me, his sister told me that her brother tried to have me killed three times, saying he knows people with the knowledge to get it done. I felt she was describing Benjamin Troy Mangum perfectly. The driver behind the colossal pick up truck that sent me to my maker.

In my deposition, I said the crash felt intentional, and I thought the driver had knowledge about what kinds of wrecks would be deadly after Jessamine's confession. In litigation, I found out the driver had a similar rear-end collision in St George in a 3/4 ton Silverado Truck. The black box was stripped clean, and the driver, Benjamin Troy Mangum, hammered out the bumper with a sledgehammer. He also never took the truck to a repair shop after the collision. Mangum claimed he was one of the only people out of many foremen at Wadman Corporation who serviced his own truck.

Mangum also had a previous job at Chevrolet that gave him the experience to know what kinds of wrecks are deadly. Mangum tried to say I intentionally braked to get a paycheck. Yet when I reported to my insurance, he agreed to my version of the story. My case went to the federal courts, which is very rare. Mike Levin would know the federal process, being a former FBI agent. Federal courts have a very short due diligence, and you have to win over all of the jurors. The wreck also happened in a shopping center parking lot, and when the driver was asked why the cops weren't called, he started reciting how cops are not called on private property. The fact he knew this was chilling.

In October of 2019, I had lunch with Farbod after I reported him and others to the FBI. I told him about all of the coincidences, showing him how Mike Levin must have been involved knowing the federal process and other coincidences tying him to the wreck. Farbod made the comment Mike must be involved.

In December of 2019, I wanted to settle with Farbod what he owed me, since the FBI agent wanted me to sue him—Farbod then started threatening my life again, saying I was going to die so quick, I wouldn't know what happened. On March 28, 2020, I got a creepy video confession from Shawn Lampman while he was at the Oasis RV Park. I was talking to my friend Jane on FaceTime when she introduced me to her friend, who she claimed was Art. I started talking to him about the book I was writing, and my near-death experience, and how I felt the wreck was tied to the pig farm. He then started taunting me right before sending the apology video.

In April of 2021, Mike Montandon sent a guy to harass me, claiming Mike Montandon was a former FBI agent, which links him to Mike Levin (another former FBI agent). Mike Levin would have been linked to Shawn Lampman through friendforfelons.org, and also, his radio show interviewing felons, which possibly gives him a criminal network.

Cased closed; this was no accident; this was meant to kill me; this has something to do with the Sattari family! I was murdered over the Hualapai and Farm escrow and also my half million dollars I leant to Bob Combs. I now have the last laugh, not the Elohim who I heard upon returning to my body or those who were behind this viscous assault.

CHAPTER 28

The Grand Picture

When I was violently murdered from this universe and returned, I became argumentative when God told me what had happened. I set out to prove him wrong. Yet when I looked for answers, I discovered that he had been right.

To this day, I find it profound that God knows all the details of all the billions of people on this earth and can see all the events that will happen in our futures. I was amazed that he could see all the intricacies of our lives. When I was dead and in that universe of pure conscious thought, I was looking at the tapestry of all of time—past, present, and future events.

Here's how I believe it works on a cosmic scale: I believe the God Force is a force of creation. Without the God Force, this universe is not possible. I know God is a conscious being. He spoke to me after my soul came back to my body. I felt the power of the God Force in his words. I felt that it was the power of the creation of this universe. When I was in that field of energy, the God Force, I had the profound feeling that I had the choice of being able to come back to life.

Elohim is the living God whose consciousness occupies the God Force, who creates this universe we're in. Jesus, Buddha, and Enoch all showed us the path to enlightenment. They all showed us how to become ascended beings. How can one achieve Godhood in the afterlife? Those whose sacred name are the Elohim.

It is an overwhelming theme of all religions to be a good person. We are judged for our actions on this earth.

The path to ascension is enlightenment, compassion, and love. It's not ignorance. It's not greed. And it's not hatred. I believe if you have these emotions in your heart when you die (ignorance, greed, and hatred) they cause you to be bound to the physical earth. We all have the spark of God within us. Immortal spiritual beings aren't able to ascend to Godhood with greed, ignorance, and hatred in their hearts. This is why I believe people come back to this earth time and time again—to eventually get it right.

My strong recommendation is to treat others how you want to be treated. Don't just treat other human beings with kindness, but *all* the creatures on the planet. They have souls too.

Based on what I've been through and my experience crossing over and coming back, I urge you to find God and love in your heart before you leave this physical universe.

If I were Elohim, and if I came across someone who left this earth who was a good person but who never believed in me, I don't think I would be willing to let that person enter my house. What happens to all the good people on this earth who don't believe in God? Do they become sons and daughters of perdition cast out into eternal darkness? That eternal pit of sorrow I gazed upon when I contemplated suicide while battling depression right after the murder attempt on my life.

All I knew when I gazed upon that portal of eternal darkness, was that it was a place I never wanted to go. What about evil people on this earth who believe in God? Are they cast into the portals of eternal darkness as well? Or are they recycled back into life? Does the pit of eternal darkness maybe even lead back to life? Only God knows the answers to these questions.

If I didn't have the near-death experience—if I had never heard the voice of God—I would be dead. God put me on high alert. With the new gift of PTSD (enhanced intuition) that God gave me, my life was saved.

· · · ·

Growing up as a child, I was never one to seek an ordinary existence. I always wanted a life of excitement and adventure. Never in a million years did I think that excitement would include being violently murdered and coming back to life to discover who was behind that failed attempt.

This realization is deeply profound on a cosmic scale. Who goes from life to death and back to life without losing any type of cognition at all? That does not happen to very many people.

When I first entered that unknown territory—the universe of pure conscious thought, the afterlife—I questioned the very existence of my soul and also of God. It was through being viciously murdered that I found both.

I realize the choices I've made that stem from a desire to seek excitement and adventure, have led me to a moment where I discovered that life is about family and not about financial success. I realized through death that greed is an earthly emotion that binds people to this earth.

One thing I had to do was get rid of anger in my heart against those people who caused me harm. I treated an adopted family and two clients I loved and cared about with kindness and generosity and was repaid with murder and fraud. In both cases, I was being lured by the possibility of huge commission checks that were never there to begin with. I bear no anger or resentment. Hate will not get you through the pearly gates.

Life isn't about how much one has over the other. Life is about relationships and how you treat other people. The greatest pleasure isn't about making a big commission check on a real estate deal; it's about helping others.

When I was dead, it literally felt as if my consciousness was hardwired into this universe. This is why I call myself a Son of Elohim. By no means do I compare myself in any way with Jesus. Jesus showed everybody on this earth what we need to do to ascend to Godhood. To become one of the Elohim.

I understand the importance of my soul. Jesus showed the correct path. I don't think you have to be a beggar in the streets to ascend, but you need to thoroughly comprehend that your possessions are not who you are. When I was dead, I realized all my material things were left behind. You don't bring those with you. You don't even bring your body with you. I was pure energy. It was only my soul that I was bringing with me into the next life. All the material things I was murdered for—they meant nothing in the afterlife.

When I came back to this physical existence, everything was different. I felt vulnerable. I felt fragile. You could see the damage on the outside and inside as I had been seriously hurt. From the shell shock, I emerged with a new sensitivity to the universe. Lights and noises were intense. I experienced a greater awareness of people, an ability to read them, that allowed me to have the enhanced intuition I needed to solve my own murder.

At first, I wanted to disbelieve the murder and prove God wrong, and that's why I assumed the mantle of detective, only to discover that God was 1,000 percent right.

Because—of course he is.

I proved God right and the experience humbled me. When I realized the truth, going through written discovery about my car wreck, I cried. It was a spiritual moment beyond any human comprehension.

At first, I thought the wreck meant I had been cursed by God. I soon realized it was a gift. It is his way of telling his story to humanity through me. It is one of the most profound of near-death experiences that I survived and am a testament to his existence.

We are in this life together. While we are here, it should be about love, compassion, and kindness.

It's about being a good person and the good you do for others. Never would God want us to fight over religion, money, or territories. He would want us all to love and get along with each other, no matter the difference in culture.

Thank you for taking the time to read my story, which is my Testament of Elohim. If you get one thing out of this book, let me repeat—treat everyone with love, compassion, and kindness in your heart, and believe in God!

Made in the USA
Columbia, SC
15 March 2024

33102107R00145